EXPLORING
DEATH VALLEY

Exploring
DEATH
VALLEY

A Guide for Tourists

by **RUTH KIRK**
photographs by **LOUIE KIRK**

STANFORD UNIVERSITY PRESS
STANFORD, CALIFORNIA

STANFORD UNIVERSITY PRESS, STANFORD, CALIFORNIA /
OXFORD UNIVERSITY PRESS, LONDON / © 1956 by the Board
of Trustees of the Leland Stanford Junior University / Printed in
the United States of America by Stanford University Press / *Library of Congress Catalog Card Number: 56-11295*

Contents

Chapter 1

The Setting

In Death Valley both events and geography tend toward the unique. Superlatives and paradoxes abound. The sink of the Valley floor is the lowest spot in the Western Hemisphere; the July temperatures are among the world's hottest; the difference in elevation between the salt flats and Telescope Peak is greater than at any other place in the United States except Mount Rainier, in Washington.

Death Valley's 140-mile trough and its bordering mountains are thought of as the epitome of dryness, yet they are better watered than most desert country. They have been reported lifeless, but actually more than six hundred species of plants are native there, and an even larger number of mammals, birds, reptiles, insects, amphibians, and fish.

The stories of the Valley, fact and folklore, portray its unique character, its spirit of individualism. Scotty's Castle is a monument to that individualism—a multimillion-dollar mansion raised in a remote canyon bordering Death Valley simply because two men wanted it there. The inconvenience of the location was not allowed to interfere. For example, to supply firewood for the Castle's 18 fireplaces Scotty's partner, A. M. Johnson, bought 120,000 ties when the Tonopah and Tidewater Railroad was torn up. He paid $1,500 for them; then he had to spend $25,000 getting them hauled to the Castle. Some have been burned, but most are neatly stacked in Tie Canyon, a draw behind the Castle.

All true Death Valley men have a touch of the same spirit that prompted the building of the Castle, a devil-may-care individualism not found in more ordinary men. There is John Thorndike, a prospector who had a winning streak gambling in Lone Pine during the turn-of-the-century mining boom, and in a surge of optimism decided to try his luck in the next town, Rhyolite. Four valleys and three mountain ranges separate the two towns, but John went, played a game, lost—and didn't think of either his bad luck or his 100-mile walk as noteworthy. Fifty years later Buck Johnson, also a prospector, set out for a lead mine with his partner, Ambroise Aguerreberry. Before they had gone far, their Model A developed a flat tire, much to Buck's annoyance. "I was restless that day," he explains. "Didn't feel like helping Ambroise patch that tire." So he cut across canyon and ridge to the mine: a 16-mile walk, round trip, with 50 pounds of ore specimens to pack out on the way back.

In the 1870's men living in the mountains west of Death Valley often had reasons for not wanting their exact whereabouts known. Their mail was addressed simply to "The Panamints," and left at a waterhole still known as Post Office Spring. In 1950, a lanky, six-footer who was staying up Trail Canyon tired of the isolation and came down to confess to Park Service Rangers that he had committed a murder in Michigan. A deputy sheriff was called and took him in custody; but on the way to jail the two stopped to attend a Christmas-week celebration at a Valley hotel. The next morning the sheriff was still sleeping it off, so the prisoner went back to Park Service headquarters and asked what to do.

Another story of sheriff and prisoner is that of Charlie Brown and Death Valley Slim, in 1907. It was Christmastime then too, and snow covered the ground at Greenwater. Slim felt like celebrating and shot up a saloon, thus putting himself in Sheriff Brown's hands. There was no jail, so Brown handcuffed the prisoner and took him to his own cabin. He locked Slim's shoes in the closet and the two stretched out on the bed, Slim still handcuffed. Both slept for a time and then Slim got up, slipped on the sheriff's size 12 shoes and departed. When Charlie Brown missed the prisoner, he had to follow him through the snow barefooted until, to use the sheriff's own words, "I found somebody with feet even bigger than mine, borrowed his shoes, and then chased Slim till I found him three miles out of town sawing off the handcuffs."

The name "Death Valley" has proved prophetic during the century that has passed since the first white men to enter the Valley gave it the only English name it has ever had. Only one white man had died there at the time, but many have died since. There is the grim record of the Lemoigne Mine, for example. The first three white men to claim its lead-silver were killed by Indians. John Lemoigne, a Frenchman, worked it after that and got along fine. Then one day on his way to Furnace Creek Ranch, he died—cause unknown. After him, W. J. Loring and a partner named Clark had the mine; Clark was killed by an automobile as he stepped off a streetcar in an Eastern city. John O'Riley then bought the mine; he died in the lobby of a Las Vegas hotel before he had finished making payments. Harry Stimler and Bill Corcoran each had it for a time. Stimler was shot to death in Tecopa; Corcoran died alone in the cave at Emigrant Spring.

The naming of the Valley was only the beginning of the somber place names. Suicide Pass, Skeleton Mine, and Poison Spring soon followed. Deadman's Gulch, Deadman's Pass, and Deadman's Mine are all named for different dead men. In the early 1900's newspapers syndicated a picture of one J. R. Wilson who worked the *graveyard* shift at the *Coffin* Mine near *Tombstone* Flat, in the *Funeral* Mountains on the eastern rim of *Death* Valley.

However, beneath the hostile veneer of Death Valley there is beauty: the vast openness of the land, the patterns of sand and salt in the Valley, the wind in the mountain pines, the hour of sundown when the heat breaks and shadows move down the Panamints and out across the desert floor.

Chapter 2

The Human Story

INDIANS

The ancient lake dwellers.—During the Ice Age a large part of Death Valley was flooded by one of a chain of lakes that covered much of the present California desert. Lake Manly (as this prehistoric lake is now called by geologists) was rimmed by terraces, at least one of which was probably the home of primitive men during a late stage of the lake—perhaps as much as 20,000 years ago. Simple tools have been found on the terrace, including stones flaked on one edge to form crude scrapers and choppers, and a few rocks that might have served as hammers. There are no arrowheads or spear points. The ancient lake dwellers were not advanced enough for such exacting workmanship.

Their way of life is conjectural, but certainly the climate they knew was much milder than that of today. The hills doubtless were fertile, and were roamed by large animals, including American lion, camel, bison, deer, and mammoth. Probably the lake dwellers were hunters and fishers roving the countryside in nomad-like bands.

Maps and petroglyphs.—The "maps" are rows of rocks laid out on Mesquite Flat, on the Cottonwood Canyon fan, and also on a fan above Emigrant Wash. One roughly suggests a many-branched tree, bare of leaves. Another resembles the outline of a house, about 20 feet across. The irregular patterns may represent a map of some sort, and for want of a better interpretation the figures are generally called "Indian maps." Their origin is unknown, but they must be very old for most of them gleam with "desert varnish" that has been produced by centuries of sunshine acting on manganese in the rocks.

Petroglyphs, or rock carvings, are found on many canyon walls—Emigrant, Cottonwood, Echo, Titus, Wildrose, and others. Often it is the contrast between the deep, satiny luster

4

of the surface patina and the lighter rock beneath that makes the figures show up. Some petroglyphs represent mountain sheep, insects, lizards, or men; others are carved in circles, wavy lines, or crosshatching. Most archaeologists believe they were made for ritual purposes. Other theories are that they point toward water or that they record incidents or illustrate stories. The present-day Indians claim to know nothing about them.

Shoshone Indians.—Fragments of baskets and pottery, occasional beads and toys, and countless arrowheads and spear-points tell of the ancestors of the modern Shoshone Indians. Archaeological relics such as these are protected by law. Sites may not be excavated nor surface material collected without permission from the Secretary of the Interior.

The early Shoshones probably drifted into the desert a band at a time. The Death Valley area was more favorable for subsistence than much of the surrounding country, but even so it took most of the Indians' time and energy to eke out a bare living, and opportunity for cultural or creative attainment was scant.

Scattered in family groups, living in simple brush houses, and moving as food supply and weather demanded, the Indians rarely had enough food stored ahead to allow them to have group gatherings. One exception was the annual circle dance held each fall after the pine nut harvest. This was the time for a whole year's ceremony and sociability. One chief (or "talker") would exhort the youths to proper behavior, while another led the men in a rabbit hunt. Rabbits, bighorn sheep, rodents, lizards, and an occasional deer furnished meat.

Cactus seeds, grass seeds, those of chia and ephedra and many other plants were painstakingly harvested and then parched by tossing with hot coals in a flat, circular basket. Pine nuts and mesquite beans were the mainstays of the Indians' diet. Pinyon pines grow in the Panamint and Grapevine ranges, and mesquites are common throughout the Valley.

The mesquite beans were picked in late June. Green-ripe pods were pounded in a mesquite-wood mortar to get juice used as a drink; dry beans were shelled by rubbing them between metate and mano stones, and then ground fine with mortar and pestle. The most prized mesquite product was a

5

candy made by winnowing a sticky white powder from the crushed beans and pods, then moistening it with water and patting it into balls which were baked in the sun.

When pine nuts ripened in the early fall, families camped among the pinyons for two or three weeks to harvest them. Men knocked cones from the trees with long poles, and women and children gathered them in bushel-size carrying baskets. The cones were then heated over coals until they popped open, releasing the oily nuts.

Some of the nuts were wrapped in hides, or in more recent times in canvas, and stored. They were generally left in the cones, uncooked, to lessen chances of rodents or coyotes digging in to them. Parched nuts were ground and mixed with water to make a mush served with meat.

The Indians today.—Five or six Indian families winter in the Valley nowadays, probably about a quarter of the number that lived there before the coming of white men. From September to May they occupy adobe houses that the government built for them south of Furnace Creek Ranch. In summer they move to the cooler elevations of Beatty and Shoshone.

Few traditions are observed any more. Mesquite beans and pine nuts ripen and fall to the ground scarcely noticed. Puberty rites and circle dances are things of the past. No medicine men are left to minister to the people's ills; the last two died in 1953. The old stories are seldom told. Almost forgotten are the accounts of why the gods were angry and flooded the Valley, forcing the people into the Panamints; of how Bighorn Sheep traveled to a distant land and brought pine nuts back to the people; and of how Rabbit once chased Sun and shot him with an arrow, making him fall from the sky and land in the mud hills near Furnace Creek.

FORTY-NINERS

The original company.—People from Illinois, Iowa, and Wisconsin on their way to the get-rich-quick California goldfields were ill prepared for Death Valley. The adventurous men and four families who were to be the first white people in the Valley belonged to the "Sand Walking" company, a name corrupted from their destination, the San Joaquin Valley. Their train of about 100 wagons was competently led by Captain Jefferson Hunt, and the trip was uneventful until they reached a point a little west of Salt Lake City. There a pack train overtook them, and the leader, O. K. Smith, showed them a short-cut map supposedly made by Walkara, a Ute chief. It was a rough sort of map and was to bring tragedy to the emigrant party. Historians think that it probably was based on Walkara's account of a horse-stealing raid he had led into California, his route illustrated by sketching in the sand while he told of his exploit. A penciled copy of this "map" is thought to be what Smith showed the Sand Walkers.

Nearly a third of the emigrants chose the new route, hoping to cut 500 miles from the established way. It was a vain and tragic hope. The "short cut" actually added six to ten weeks to their odyssey, a time later summed up by Mrs. Brier, one of the party, as "always the same—hunger and thirst and an awful silence."

The Jayhawker company.—Among the Sand Walkers who decided to try the short cut was a band of young men who called themselves the Jayhawkers. For them, Death Valley was no harder than the rest of the desert. A log kept by Sheldon Young, a member of the band, notes tersely that it was hot Christmas Day, 1849, when they entered the Valley; but the two or three days they spent plodding across it were little distinguished from the other weary, often waterless days in the desert. Most of the Jayhawkers entered the then-nameless Valley by way of what is now known as Furnace Creek Wash. They wandered north to the Salt Creek area, and there burned their wagons and smoked the meat of their remaining oxen preparatory to leaving the Valley on foot through Townes Pass and Jayhawker Canyon.

The Rev. J. W. Brier, his wife, and their small sons aged four, seven, and nine traveled with the Jayhawkers much of the way although they did not belong to the original group. Their ordeal is made the more touching by the illness of Rev. Brier, who lost a hundred pounds during the desert crossing, and by the exceptional heroism of his wife. "Many times when night came," she wrote, "my husband would be on ahead looking for water, and I would search, on my hands and knees, in the starlight for tracks of the oxen. . . . Poor little Kirk . . . would stumble on the salty marsh for a time and then sink down crying 'I can't go any farther!' and then I would carry him . . ."

7

The Bennett-Arcane party.—The main forty-niner story belongs to the Bennett and Arcane families, for in their memories Death Valley was tragically distinguished from the rest of the desert. (Members of the Arcane family probably spelled their name "Arcan," but it is usually written now "Arcane.")

Instead of following the Jayhawkers north through the Valley, the seven wagons of the Bennett-Arcane party turned south and camped at one of the springs at the foot of the Panamints, probably Tule Spring. There they took stock of their plight. Lost, and with little food left, they decided to send two young men ahead to scout the way to the settlements that they believed lay just over the Panamints.

William Manly and John Rogers agreed to go. Their trip from Death Valley to near San Fernando proved much longer and harder than they expected, but even so, their one thought on reaching the settlement was to return to the stricken party waiting for them in the desert. Ranchers gave them two horses and a one-eyed mule packed with provisions, and a Mexican woman sent oranges to the children. The two men started back over the dread 250 miles, leading the animals. The horses died on the way, but the mule kept on.

Between three and four weeks after their departure from the Valley Manly and Rogers again entered it. They found that the eight single men accompanying the Bennetts and Arcanes had struck out on their own. Only the two families awaited the scouts' return.

They quickly began the long trip out of the Valley. The second day they topped the Panamints and, according to Manly's own account, turned to look back and say, "Good-bye, Death Valley." Twenty-one days later they dragged themselves to the San Francisquito Ranch, a 700,000-acre land grant owned by Don Antonio del Valle.

Nearly two months had passed since the emigrants entered Death Valley. Twenty-seven wagons went into the Valley; one came out. It belonged to the Wades, a family of five who camped near the Bennetts and Arcanes for a time and then turned south and made their way to San Bernardino without undue hardship.

The only death in the Valley itself was that of Captain Robert Culverwell, one of those who wandered off from the

Bennett-Arcane camp. He died alone somewhere on the fan west of where Eagle Borax Works were to operate a quarter of a century later.

PROSPECTORS

Panamint City.—Not many years after they struggled out of the Valley, some of the forty-niners went back to prospect. One of the Jayhawkers had picked up a chunk of silver ore while looking for a lost gunsight, and his find touched off a wave of mining enthusiasm that has not abated with the passing of more than a century.

The first boom town, Panamint City, was tucked in a canyon high in the mountains west of Death Valley, where a silver chloride strike was made in 1873. Eighteen months after the strike a full-fledged town of 1,000 had sprung up, complete with newspaper, saloons, and girls imported from San Francisco's Barbary Coast. Fresh vegetables were packed in from Hungry Bill's Ranch, ten miles away over the Panamints; and other supplies were hauled by wagon from Los Angeles. At that time the City of the Angels had just established its role as the metropolis of southern California by having underbid Ventura for the trade of Cerro Gordo, a mining camp in the Inyo Mountains, and its merchants therefore welcomed Panamint City's business as a chance to strengthen their lead.

Some ore assayed as high as $4,000 a ton, and after it was displayed in a Los Angeles bar two million dollars' worth of stock was successfully floated by the Panamint Mining Company. By 1877, however, Senators John P. Jones and William M. Stewart, who backed the company, had suffered a loss equal to the initial stock issue—although, as writer Bourke Lee put it, "many other millions were handed around between the beginning and the end."

Aaron and Rosie.—In 1873 the *Inyo Independent* reported the discovery of borax in Death Valley. Borax had first been found in the United States only a few years earlier, in northern California, and with a going price of about 35 cents a pound it opened up a promising new aspect of the nation's mineral wealth.

Eight years after the newspaper report a prospector happened by Aaron and Rosie Winters' hovel in Ash Meadows, east of the Funeral Mountains. He talked of borax, and in the course of the evening not only described its appearance but mentioned that it burned green when moistened with sulphuric acid and alcohol.

Aaron and Rosie listened carefully, then set out for Furnace Creek. What they had seen in the marsh near there fitted the description of borax, and they wanted to mix some of it with acid and alcohol and see the color of its flame. They gathered a little of the soft white stuff that was leached out of the marsh—"cottonball borax"—and in a few moments Aaron's "She burns green, Rosie—we're rich!" ushered in the era that put Death Valley on the map.

The 20-mule team.—Winters sent a sackful of borax to William T. Coleman, a San Francisco entrepreneur who had backed a borax operation in Nevada. Coleman responded by sending representatives to Death Valley authorized to purchase the Winters' interests for $20,000. Aaron and Rosie were overjoyed. Coleman organized a company that eventually became the Pacific Coast Borax Company.

Harmony Borax Works was set up a mile north of Furnace Creek Ranch; borax refining began in 1882. Indians were hired to cut mesquite for the boilers under the crystallizing vats, and Chinese coolies working in mid-valley gathered baskets of the cottonball borax in baskets and hauled it to Harmony on sledges. When May came, the thermometer soared and borax would not crystallize on the iron rods suspended in the vat. Harmony had to close for the summer, and operations were transferred to the Amargosa Works, south of Shoshone, at an elevation high enough for summer crystallizing.

It was there that the 20-mule team idea was born. Coleman had hired Charles Bennett, an Ash Meadows rancher unrelated to the forty-niner Bennett family, and his eight-mule team and wagon to haul borax from the Harmony plant. When the Amargosa Works started up, Bennett was joined by another driver, Ed Stiles, who had hauled for the Eagle Borax Works during the brief time it had processed borax in southern Death Valley. Stiles had twelve mules, and the Amargosa foreman noticed that they handled twice the load of the smaller team. If twelve mules could do double the work

Twenty-Mule Team

INDIANS

Susie Wilson

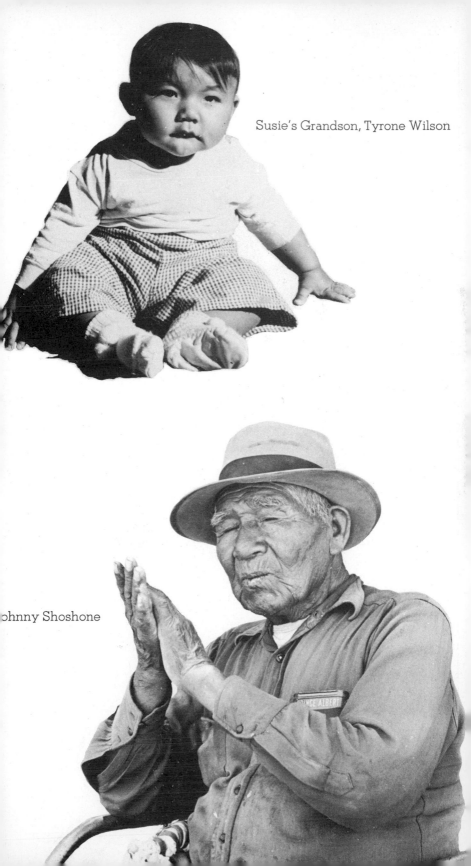

Susie's Grandson, Tyrone Wilson

ohnny Shoshone

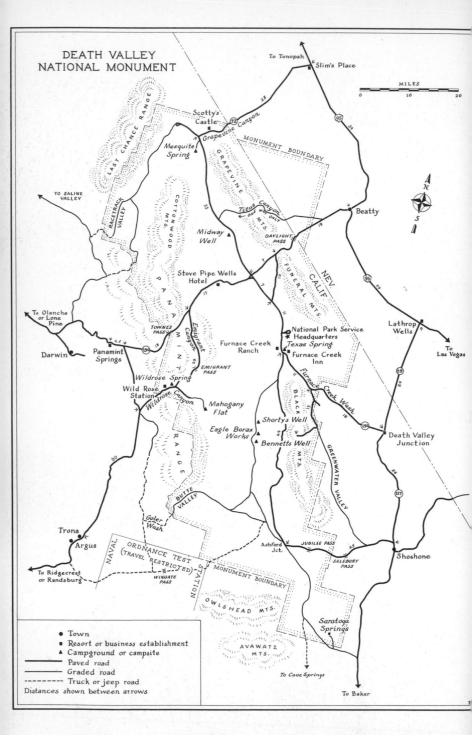

DEATH VALLEY
NATIONAL MONUMENT

Legend:
- ● Town
- ■ Resort or business establishment
- ▲ Campground or campsite
- Paved road
- Graded road
- ------ Truck or jeep road
- Distances shown between arrows

ROUTES, ACCOMMODATIONS, AND CAMPGROUNDS

Devils Cornfield

Creosote bush

ANIMALS

Above: Horned Toad

Below: Gecko Lizard

Above: Pack Rat

Below: Chuckwalla Lizard

Above: A scorpion stings a cricket before eating it

Below: Red racer snakes, like most snakes, are harmless

of eight, he reasoned, why wouldn't all twenty put together haul a really big load?

The idea proved sound. Special wagons were ordered to fit the capacity of the mules. They were built sixteen feet long, four feet wide, and six feet deep. Empty they weighed nearly four tons. A full load of two wagons and a 1,200-gallon water tank weighed 36½ tons. The rig was powerful but slow; the 165-mile haul from Death Valley to the railhead at Mojave took ten days, but the wagons served without breakdown for the five years they were needed. They still stand intact at Furnace Creek Ranch.

Turn-of-the-century boom towns.—Death Valley became a prospectors' mecca for both minerals and metallics. Claims were staked one day, and towns developed the next. A 1908 issue of the *Rhyolite Herald* assured its readers that Death Valley's "borders are lined with precious metals. Gold, silver, copper, lead, and all manner of metals are found here. An expert has even declared the presence of diamonds. Its salt and borax deposits are the most extensive in the world."

One excitement merged into the next: the Keane Wonder; Rhyolite; Chloride City; Greenwater; Harrisburg. Millions of dollars were poured into the ground, and for a time millions in gold and silver came back out.

The town of Rhyolite had the most spectacular growth of all. In 1904, when Shorty Harris cut his pick into a chunk of green-speckled gold ore and named his strike "The Bullfrog," there was scarcely another white man within fifty miles. Less than two years later a town of over 5,000 grew up almost on the spot. Rhyolite had a three-story hotel, a bank, a $20,000 school, two railway depots, a stock exchange, and two churches, as well as the inevitable mining camp bars and dance halls.

Regular stage service was maintained from Rhyolite to Skidoo, across the Valley, and there was a telephone line between them. Bullfrog, South Bullfrog, South Circle, and Brawn City grew up around Rhyolite. Chloride City and Keane Wonder lay between Rhyolite and Skidoo. Harrisburg was a tent city near Skidoo, in the Panamints. Greenwater flourished in the Black Mountains, Schwaub and Lee in the Funerals.

There were four or five boom years, then suddenly a market panic. Investors were scared off, mines closed, and people left.

RANGERS

By the 1920's official government explorations and unofficial prospecting expeditions had supplanted the forty-niners' tales of woe with reports of fantastic wealth and beauty. Roads were bad, but tourists were already discovering Death Valley.

In 1933 the Valley and its bordering ranges were set aside by presidential proclamation as Death Valley National Monument, part of the National Park system of areas preserved for their scenic, scientific, or historic value. Death Valley rates high in all three categories: scenically, as a magnificent example of desert wilderness; scientifically, as an area of exceptionally varied geologic interest and as the home of bighorn sheep and other animals, and plants, once native throughout much of the desert but now often hard-pressed for survival; and historically, as the setting of a poignant chapter in the pioneers' westward push, and as part of the story of Western mining.

Death Valley is the second largest unit in the United States National Park System. (Death Valley National Monument encompasses 1,907,720 acres; Yellowstone National Park, 2,221,773 acres.) The system is administered by the National Park Service under congressional direction to "conserve the scenery and the natural and historic objects therein." The program is twofold: to help the public understand and appreciate the area as part of the national heritage, and to protect the area from commercial exploitation and vandalism. To carry out this program the Monument is in the immediate charge of a superintendent, assisted by a staff that includes the rangers and naturalists familiar to all National Park visitors, as well as clerks, laborers, and specialists. Regulations in Death Valley, as in other National Park areas, stipulate that historic sites shall not be disturbed, animals molested, plants removed or damaged, or rocks collected without the specific permission of the superintendent.

Chapter 3

Natural History

ROCKS

The time concept.—Time in terms of millions of years is beyond mental grasp, but that is the length of time that has shaped the earth. The astronomer Jeans has expressed the concept by saying that if the height of the Woolworth Building is taken to represent the length of geologic history, "we may lay a nickel on its tower to represent the span of human existence on Earth and a thin sheet of paper upon this to represent all historic time."

Geologists estimate the earth's age at from two billion to five billion years, and the earth is still changing. Some physical features were produced ages ago; some belong to today. Death Valley has rocks representing the entire span of geologic time.

Rocks from the most ancient era, the Archeozoic, may be seen in the Black Mountains, along the road to Badwater. Some show signs of "bedding planes," indicating that much of the range originated as sediment laid down at the bottom of a shallow sea.

The next oldest rocks, the Proterozoic, probably were also deposited at the bottom of a sea. Harrisburg Flat is surrounded by rocks dating from that era, and Mosaic Canyon cuts through Proterozoic marble.

The Paleozoic era, the third oldest, began about 500 million years ago. Fossil-bearing rocks belonging to it are generally a somber gray; some are conspicuously banded. Striped Butte is made up of Paleozoic sediments; and the rocks at Aguerreberry Point and in lower Titus Canyon date from this era.

Granites are the chief representatives in Death Valley of the fourth era, the Mesozoic. Cottonwood Canyon, north of the Townes Pass road, is formed in Mesozoic rock, and so is much of the Skidoo area, in the Panamints.

The present era, the Cenozoic, which began about 60 million years ago, is the most widely represented in the Valley. The colorful rocks of the Grapevine Mountains date from it; Mushroom Rock is Cenozoic basalt; the tawny hills at Zabriskie Point are the upended and eroded beds of lakes that belong to this era, as do the still-forming alluvial fans, the Sand Dunes, and the playas such as the Racetrack.

The shaping of Death Valley.—Several times Death Valley has been under a sea, then uplifted into mountains, worn away to a plain, and again covered with water. The Valley as it is today began forming in late Cenozoic time, probably not over a million years ago. It is a "structural valley," or "fault basin"—one of a series of mountain-walled troughs comprising what geologists call the "Basin and Range Province," which is characteristic of much of the Southwest.

Death Valley was formed by stresses in the earth's crust that uplifted the mountains on each side and dropped the floor of the valley. The process was not sudden or simple, nor is it necessarily complete. Obvious examples of the folding, faulting, tilting, and eroding that have sculptured the area are scattered throughout the Monument. The forces were so complex and mixed in places that one geologist, despairing of untangling the structural story, dubbed Death Valley an "eggbeater formation—some of this and some of that mixed beyond recognition."

Some interesting features.—Among the common geologic features are fault scarps, which are cliffs resulting from fractures and dislocations in the earth's crust. One such scarp is on the Hanaupah fan, along the eastern foot of the Panamints. It is as much as 30 feet high. A much smaller but more accessible fault scarp is near the mouth of Golden Canyon just south of Furnace Creek Inn.

Volcanic rocks are widespread. Ubehebe Crater and the half-dozen other explosion craters in the northern Valley are the most obvious representatives. The peculiarly shaped black hill west of Furnace Creek Ranch, "The Dinosaur," is the result of basalt flows; ridges of volcanic rock called dikes are found in several places, most noticeably near Rhodes Well, in the Jubilee Pass area.

Lakes once were a prominent feature. At least two lakes flooded the Valley during the Pleistocene period, or Ice Age, of the present era: Lake Rogers, evidenced today by the white sediments north of Ubehebe Crater, and Lake Manly, a larger lake that covered the southern Valley to an estimated depth of 600 feet. Wave-cut beaches are readily noticeable in several places: Shoreline Butte, in the extreme southern end of Death Valley; Manly Terrace, a little north of Badwater; and at a point a mile and a half beyond State Highway 190, where the southern approach road to Daylight Pass cuts through a low ridge of water-worn cobbles. The salt on the Devils Golf-course, in the central Valley, was left when Lake Manly dried.

Lake beds that predate Lake Manly are found along the western foot of the Black Mountains at such places as 20-Mule Team Canyon, Zabriskie Point, and Golden Canyon; lakes far more recent are the playas, or "dry lakes," found in and near the Monument today, such as the Racetrack and the Bonnie Claire.

The alluvial fans spilling from the mountains onto the Valley floor are another physiographic feature produced by water. These immense debris deposits erode from the mountains and accumulate in fan-shaped slopes at the canyon mouths. The greater size of the fans in the Panamint and Cottonwood ranges, compared with those of the Grapevine and Funeral and Black mountains, indicates that the eastern rim of the Valley has been dislocated more recently than the western rim. The dark tones of some fans indicate material that has lain undisturbed long enough to build up surface patina, or "desert varnish," while pale grays and tans represent debris recently washed down from the mountains.

Among the other geologic features of the Monument are the sand dunes, produced by eddying winds; the "hour-glass" canyons, so called because of their wide drainage basins, narrow outlets, and enormous debris slopes; the polished breccia, or natural mosaic, of Mosaic Canyon; desert pavement, with its close-set stones looking as smooth and firm as a highway; and the "moving rocks" that skid across the Racetrack Playa, evidently blown by the wind.

ANIMALS

Desert adaptation.—Death Valley animals are widely scattered according to the ability of the land to support them.

A seed-eater is limited to the locale of favored plants, a flesh-eater to that of suitable prey. An animal must have a range that is large and fairly free of competitors in order to get enough food.

Most desert creatures get along on almost no water. Many never touch standing water, and others wait a long time between drinks. Rodents adjust to excessive heat and scant water better than other mammals. During the daytime, they usually stay underground where temperatures are about 15 degrees cooler. Few perspire; many pass but little urine. Several are able to get water from the carbohydrates in the seeds they eat.

Birds get much of their needed moisture from succulent leaves and berries, or from the blood of insects, lizards, and rabbits. In years of scant food, wrens and thrashers may nest earlier than usual and lay fewer eggs, or even forego nesting altogether.

Insects, particularly in larval and pupal stages, wait out adverse conditions by going into a dormant state until normal life may feasibly be resumed. The eggs of some survive great heat and drought, hatching only when rain moistens them, much as seeds await conditions that favor germination. The naturalist Edmund C. Jaeger tells of some springtail eggs, which usually hatch in a little over a week, taking as long as 271 days to hatch when dried.

Animals to watch for.—Lizards are more frequently seen than other forms of wildlife. Gridiron-tailed lizards streak across the highway in front of cars, and brown swifts often dart from underfoot. Whiptails are seen both on the Valley floor and in the mountains, snapping up ants and other tiny insects with their long tongues. Horned toads (which really are lizards, not toads) spend much of their time buried in the sand showing only their snub-nosed, armor-crowned heads. Chuckwallas are the largest lizards in the Monument, 12 to 15 inches long. The gecko is another lizard occasionally seen, a fragile-looking creature with a pink-brown, waxy skin and a thick tail; it has the curious habit of squeaking when disturbed—the only lizard with a voice.

Two rattlesnakes, the sidewinder and the Panamint rattler, are the only poisonous creatures in the Monument. They are seldom seen. A rattler sunning on a rock or a sidewinder resting half-buried in the sand of a wash usually will get away when disturbed, but if startled it may strike, with or without its characteristic warning buzz. About 15 species of snakes are found in the Monument.

None of the insects in the Monument, or the related scorpions, centipedes, and spiders, are deadly poisonous and few are annoying. Scorpions hide under rocks by day and forage for insects by night. Their sting is painful but not serious. (The only poisonous scorpions in the United States are found in southern Arizona.) Centipedes and tarantulas are not common in Death Valley. The most likely pest is the inch-long horsefly.

Furnace Creek Ranch generally is the best place to watch for birds. Several years ago Joseph Grinnell counted 232 individual birds of various species there in three hours. They are to be seen in the athel and mesquite trees and in the marsh behind the golf course. Bluebirds, robins, blackbirds, Say phoebes, Audubon warblers, sparrows, meadowlarks, and mourning doves are common at certain times of the year. Cinnamon teal, killdeer, and Wilson's snipe may be seen in the marsh. About 25 species of waterbirds have been reported, most of them seen only during migration. The mallard, Canada goose, great blue heron, glossy ibis, and snowy egret sometimes settle for a night or two at the Ranch and other places where there are marshes. Ravens are often seen in the Monument, particularly along highways where they watch for carrion; and marsh hawks, red tails, and occasionally eagles circle overhead, watching for lizards and rodents. A total of 240 bird species have been found in the Monument.

Mammals are less common than other types of wildlife. Antelope ground squirrels often are seen, almost the only mammals scampering about on a hot summer day. Over one-third of the 40 mammals on the National Park Service list are mice and rats. There are wood rats and kangaroo rats, pocket mice and harvest mice. Bats comprise the next largest group, making up about 15 per cent of the total species. Rabbits and squirrels each have three representatives. Bobcats, badgers, coyotes, kitfoxes, bighorn sheep, and wild burros are also on the list. Animals of rabbit size and smaller greatly outnumber larger ones, both in species represented and total population.

PLANTS

Adaptations.—Desert plants must first get water, and then conserve it, sometimes for long periods between rains. Adaptations such as small leaves and far-reaching roots partially solve the problem. Some plants send their roots deep; others develop shallow, radiating root systems. Mesquite roots have been known to penetrate as deep as 100 feet, while an 18-inch cholla cactus may have a root network that lies close to the surface of the ground and measures 20 feet across.

Many desert plants develop small leaves to reduce the water loss of transpiration. The total leaf surface of an acre of Death Valley plants probably would be less than that of an ordinary sycamore tree. Little-leaf ratany, dalea, and burrobush have quarter-inch leaves; and they are not exceptional in size. Few desert leaves measure over half an inch square. Mormon tea has nothing but scales for leaves, the twigs carrying on the normal work of leaves. Cacti have no leaves, the green-skinned stems taking over the functions of the leaf organs. Cassia drops its leaves during summer droughts. Creosote bushes and desert fir leaves are coated with resin to reduce transpiration. Brittlebush and Death Valley sage leaves are covered with hairy mats which provide insulation for the plant, an important factor since living protoplasm cannot endure temperatures much over 120 degrees Fahrenheit.

With an altitude range of over 11,000 feet and soil conditions varying from salty marshes to sand dunes, the Monument offers many growing conditions. The salt flats are bordered with pickleweed, iodine bush, and honeysweet. Out of the salt marsh area, but still influenced by it, are arrowweed and salt grass, followed by mesquite and shadscale. Then come greasewood and the beginning of a zone characterized by creosote bush, desert holly, and burrobush. This belt is a wide one. It climbs well into the mountains before merging into stands of sagebrush and rabbit bush, which in turn give way to pinyon pines and junipers.

Within their altitude range, plants indicate the amount and type of water available. Nearly a hundred species of reeds and bushes grow in water or wet soil; pickleweed and salt grass grow where brackish water is close to the surface; and tules and arrowweed also grow close to water that may be of poor quality. Fern, seepwillow bushes, athel, and cottonwood trees grow where fresh water, or slightly brackish water is readily available. Watercress chokes an occasional mountain stream or spring. Thornbush, sweetbush, and arrowleaf grow on dry hillsides.

Trees.—Death Valley National Monument provides proper growing conditions for over a dozen native trees. In addition there are athels, widely naturalized; fruit and nut trees, set out in the 1870's at a mountain ranch; and palm trees at Furnace Creek Ranch, which yield tons of dates each year. The number of species makes an impressive list for Death Valley; but the number of individuals is not great. Only the mesquites in the Valley proper and the pinyons and junipers above 6,500 feet are truly abundant.

The feathery gray-green trees at the Ranch and Park Service headquarters are athels. Mahogany Flat is named for the mountain mahogany growing there. The trail to Telescope Peak passes among bristlecone and limber pines, some of which measure three feet through the trunk. Cottonwoods shade a flowing stream in a canyon north of Townes Pass, and are seen at Wild Rose Station and Scotty's Castle and at many mountain springs.

Willows are another tree that often grow near springs. The highway circles a large willow thicket at the Y in Wildrose Canyon, and they grow at Daylight Spring. Rocky Mountain maple and water birch are to be found in remote Panamint Mountain canyons reached by hiking. Joshua trees dot the west side of Tin Mountain, on the way to the Racetrack, and the flat near Nemo Canyon, west of the highway through the Panamints. Smoketrees grow near the southern end of the Valley.

Bushes.—Over six hundred species of plants grow in the Valley and surrounding mountains. The creosote bush probably characterizes the Monument and the entire Southwest desert more than any other. It is a lacy bush, sometimes head-high, with shiny green leaves and bright yellow flowers—a sharp contrast to the gray that predominates in desert plants.

Many bushes are hard to identify except during their brief leafing and flowering periods. Desert holly is an exception. Its sharply scalloped, silvery leaves remain the year round. In early spring tiny red buds that look like berries burst from the stem tips. Brittlebush is another gray perennial readily iden-

19

tified. It grows in washes as a rounded clump with yellow, daisy-like blooms borne on long flower stalks.

Common among the scrubby gray bushes are burrobush, dalea, cheesebush, sagebrush, shadscale, and saltbush. The scraggly pickleweed is the most salt-tolerant of Death Valley plants. It grows as a low tangle of dusty green and brown stems that are jointed like a string of tiny, fat pickles. Badwater and the Devils Cornfield are good places to find it. Erect, leafless, yellow-green and gray-green clumps of Mormon tea are frequent in the Monument.

Bushes that are frequent in washes include wetleaf, a two-foot plant with bright green leaves that are moist to the touch no matter how hot the day; paper bag bush, a rounded shrub with seed pods like half-inch, papery balloons; stingbush, growing in rock crevices, a foot or two high with barbed, stinging hairs covering its leaves; desert rue, which has leathery, leafless green stems; and cigarette-holder bush, or desert trumpet, with oddly inflated stems that spring from a low tuft of leaves.

Cactus.—Countless Death Valley plants are spiny, but true cactus is not widespread. Cottontop cactus is probably more noticeable than any other, especially in the Panamints. It grows in clumps of from three or four up to ten or twelve melon-sized heads that are covered with stout, pink thorns. Cotton-like tufts encase the seeds.

Beavertail cactus grows on many hillsides, glowing with magenta flowers in spring. Cholla and hedgehog cacti are found along the road to Daylight Pass; and grizzly bear cactus grows in the high Panamints, its small pads shaggy with three- to five-inch white spines. Fishhook and corkseed cactus grow in the high mountains—single pineapple-like heads with long, hooked thorns surrounded by shorter radial spines. The most colorful flowering species is mound cactus, a rounded cushion of from six to sixty heads covered with scarlet blossoms. It is found in upper Wildrose Canyon, and elsewhere in the mountains. The best "cactus garden" in the Monument is probably that south of Ubehebe Crater, along the road leading to the Racetrack.

Wildflowers.—Annuals cover the washes and fans following as little as two inches of well-distributed winter rain and snow. However, many years fail to produce that much moisture. Daylight Pass and Jubilee Pass usually have the best display of spring flowers. Yellow desertgold brightens roadsides, and white "gravel ghost" flowers seem to hover stemless above the desert floor. Phacelia, sand verbena, and lupine color the ground with purple; evening primroses add yellow and white; and Indian paintbrush and apricot mallow lend touches of red and orange.

In some years the wildflowers bloom as early as February, but usually the best displays in the Valley are in March and April. Mountain plants often blossom throughout the summer.

Chapter 4

Weather

THE FACTS

Temperatures.—Temperature and precipitation data are regularly recorded in Death Valley, and special studies of radiation, evaporation, humidity, and wind are made from time to time. Temperatures are taken at National Park Service headquarters and at Furnace Creek Ranch in standard Weather Bureau louvered boxes set five feet above the ground. No regular readings have been made on the below-sea-level salt flats, but maximums there would be higher than those recorded to date at the present weather stations.

Death Valley summer temperatures are consistently higher than those recorded anywhere else in the world. Maximums of 120 degrees Fahrenheit were reached each July except one during a ten-year period, from 1943 to 1952. During more than half of those months it reached or exceeded 125 degrees.

The world's maximum reading is reported from North Africa, at Azizia, Libya, where a reading of 136 degrees was taken. However, the average summer temperatures there are about 10 per cent cooler than the averages at Death Valley; and the Valley's highest temperature to date is only two degrees lower than Azizia's record high. Death Valley's record was reached in July 1913 when temperatures ran at least 127 degrees for more than a week, and three times exceeded 130 degrees.

Every month except November, December, January, and February has produced temperatures over 100 degrees, and each of these winter months has reached 85 degrees at least once since systematic observations were begun in 1911. Temperatures climbed above 100 degrees on 113 consecutive days in 1953, except for two days in August.

Standard temperatures do not tell the whole story. Thermometers placed on the ground, in the shade, commonly record from 20 to 40 degrees above the air temperature; 180-

degree temperatures have been recorded in this way. Air temperatures inside a car sometimes climb to 140 degrees in summer.

On a July day in 1949 the minimum temperature failed to drop below 98 degrees, although July lows average around 88. January minimums are close to 40 degrees, and freezing temperatures may occur from October through March. In January 1937, the temperature on 21 days dropped below freezing, but the January average between 1935 and 1955 was only three freezes. Nine of those years never recorded 32 degrees during January. In 1913, when the 134-degree, high reading was taken, the January to July temperature range was 119 degrees. Death Valley's record cold was reached that same year, on January 8, when there was a drop to 15 degrees above zero.

On most winter days the weather is pleasant, although it can be hot or cold. The usual November to March midday temperature averages between 65 and 75 degrees; nights generally run from 40 to 50.

Humidity, rain and snow.—Moisture in the air is extremely low. No prolonged, systematic study of humidity has been made, but both dew point and relative humidity readings have approached zero on occasional July days, and readings of 2 and 3 per cent are frequent. In summer the relative humidity probably averages between 5 and 20 per cent, while in winter readings from 30 to 50 per cent may be expected on cloudless days. By contrast, the average relative humidity for Los Angeles is 68 per cent, and for the nation, 72 per cent. The effects of Death Valley's dry air are numerous: wood shrinks, causing nails to loosen and cabinet joints to come apart, corks dry up and fall into bottles, and paper turns brittle.

Three days out of four are cloudless in Death Valley. Only one in ten is overcast. It would take almost a century for Death Valley rainfall to total the amount averaged yearly at stations on the Olympic Peninsula. Moisture evaporates in the hot, dry air over Death Valley; less than two inches a year reach its floor. Occasionally long streamers of rain may be seen leaving clouds but not reaching the ground. The number of rainy days per year between 1942 and 1952 ranged from 6 to 28 and averaged 16.

Cloudbursts are frequent in summer but seldom are measured because they are extremely localized. An inch of rain may fall within an hour or two on a mountain slope while perhaps five miles away there will be only a trace of rain, or none at all. A 1950 cloudburst brought water and rock down Furnace Creek Wash to cut the pavement as much as six and eight feet in places and blanket it with up to four feet of silt and gravel. Yet at Park Service headquarters, four miles north, only 0.08 inch of rain was recorded.

The Titus Canyon road washes out almost every summer. Surprise Canyon's large drainage basin and narrow outlet make it similarly susceptible to cloudburst damage. Panamint City was washed out of upper Surprise Canyon in the 1870's. One day ore shipments were made as usual; the next, pieces of the buildings from the upper canyon were strewn along the road in the lower canyon, washed out by a cloudburst. Years later two prospectors worked the old Panamint claims, packing ore out on burros and rebuilding the road a little at a time. After 18 years of intermittent work the road was passable for a truck, but a cloudburst washed the road out after they had driven to the mine only twice.

Snow covers the Panamints from December to May, with drifts sometimes reaching 20 feet. Occasionally the road over Townes Pass or across Harrisburg Flat is blocked by snow. Winter snowstorms sometimes blow across the Valley from the mountains, the flakes melting as they land. In 1949 four inches stayed on the Valley floor for several hours.

EFFECT OF HEAT ON MAN

The need for water.—The normal deep body-temperature is about 98.6 degrees. Any heat rise above that must be dissipated or fever and impaired efficiency will result. Normal skin temperature is 92 degrees. When the air is warmer than that, the body can lose excess heat only by "evaporative cooling"—sweating. The dry atmosphere in Death Valley makes sweat evaporate immediately, leaving a salty grit on the skin.

Sweat is composed almost entirely of water. When increased body heat requires sweating, the water used to cool the body must be replaced. Thirst, therefore, is a signal of need, not merely a matter of comfort. In fact, the desire for water usually lags behind the actual need. With the temperature at 110 degrees, a man driving a car may sweat almost one quart of water an hour, and will need to drink an equivalent amount in order to maintain body efficiency.

Loss of body salt through sweating may contribute to heat distress. However, physiologists no longer recommend salt tablets except in cases where heavy muscular activity is required in extremely high temperatures, such as for steelworkers, glassworkers, and deep miners. An above-normal concentration of salt in the body fluids, requires water to eliminate the excess salt, and thereby to some extent deprives the body of water for sweat production. Seasoning food with a little extra salt is generally the best way to replenish the salt loss during hot weather.

Desert survival.—Sweating produces measurable decreases in body weight due to water loss. A drop equivalent to as little as 2 per cent can result in heat distress. For a 150-pound man this would mean a loss of three pounds, or about one and a half quarts of sweat. When dehydration produces a 15 to 20 per cent drop in weight it usually becomes fatal.

In addition to thirst, the discomforts of dehydration include a feeling of heat oppression and headache, muscular fatigue, rising body temperature and pulse rate, and a tingling sensation in arms and legs.

When walking becomes necessary under extremely hot desert conditions, it should be done at night. By walking eight hours a night, starting about 10:00 P.M. when temperatures have dropped, one can go nearly three times as far with a given amount of water as would be possible by walking during the daytime. Days should be spent in the shade, sheltered from drying winds and lying down to facilitate blood circulation. Clothes should be kept on to reduce the body heat gain from sun and ground radiation and from air movement. Loose clothing is desirable because it interferes less with sweat evaporation than close-fitting clothing, and therefore is cooler. Nothing should be eaten, except perhaps a little candy, because the digestion of food diverts water from sweat production. The old tales of thirst-crazed men drinking blood may be true, but doing so would cause a reduction in the water available for body cooling. If water or another liquid not suitable for drinking is available, it may be used for body cooling by wetting the clothes, thus for a time reducing the need to evaporate sweat.

In the 1900's men crossing Death Valley from one mining camp to another during the summer sometimes died of dehydration and exposure. Today, however, with good roads and fast cars and the watchful eye of National Park Service rangers, travelers cross the Valley even in mid-summer without difficulty. Suggestions for hot weather travel are posted at each entrance to the Monument. Rangers emphasize that if trouble develops there is no reason to feel panic: simply drink plenty of water, keep out of the sun, and stay with the car until help comes.

The great majority of Death Valley travelers, visiting the Monument between October and May, will experience delightful weather.

Chapter 5

Where to Stay

HOTELS AND CABINS

Inside the Monument

Furnace Creek Inn.—Open from about Veterans Day (November 11) to Easter. Located on State Highway 190 in the central Valley. Elevation, sea level. American plan; accommodates 135 guests.

Furnace Creek Inn is a luxury hotel with striking architecture and landscaping. A barber shop and beauty shop, gift shop, cocktail lounge, and dining room are situated within the hotel. Separate quarters and dining room are available for guests' servants. There is a garage with mechanic and towing services across the highway from the Inn. Tennis courts and a warm, spring-fed swimming pool are available free to guests, and at a nominal charge to others. Inn guests are not charged greens fees at the Furnace Creek Ranch golf course. Park Service naturalists conduct evening lecture programs at the Inn several times a week during the winter season.

Address inquiries to Fred Harvey Hotels, 530 West 6th Street, Los Angeles 14.

Furnace Creek Ranch.—Open from mid-October through April; service station operated year round. Located on State 190 in Central Death Valley. Elevation 178 feet below sea level. European plan; accommodations for 350 guests, ranging from sleeping cabins without bath to four-room housekeeping cottages.

The Ranch was founded as headquarters for the 20-mule team when the near-by Harmony Borax Works was processing borax. A date orchard was set out in the 1920's and tourist accommodations were added. Wagons and mine equipment used half a century and more ago are on the Ranch grounds, and a small museum houses displays of Death Valley history.

A dining room serves full-course meals at breakfast, lunch,

and dinner; a snack bar serves sandwiches, coffee, cold drinks, and ice cream. A grocery store and gift shop are in the main Ranch building; a service station is across the road. Swimming pool, nine-hole golf course, and saddle horses are on the grounds. A paved, CAA-approved airport is adjacent. Park Service naturalists conduct evening lecture programs in the recreation hall several times a week, and regularly scheduled movies are shown. Occasionally there is a dance.

Address inquiries to Fred Harvey Hotels, 530 West 6th Street, Los Angeles 14.

Scotty's Castle.—Open year round. Located in northern Death Valley. Elevation 3,000 feet. European plan, with breakfast included in lodging rates; accommodates 35 guests.

The Castle is situated in a canyon cutting through the Grapevine Mountains into northern Death Valley. Snacks are available as well as full-course meals; there is a service station on the grounds. Tours through the Castle (small fee) are conducted hourly from 9:00 A.M. to 5:00 P.M. during the main travel season, and according to demand the rest of the year. The Castle is well located for travelers entering or leaving Death Valley by Grapevine Canyon, the northernmost pass in regular use.

Address inquiries to Scotty's Castle, P.O. Box 657, Goldfield, Nevada.

Stove Pipe Wells Hotel.—Open from October until June; service station open year round. Located on State 190 in the north central Valley, near the Sand Dunes. Elevation sea level. European plan; accommodations for 100 guests.

In the main hotel building, near the lobby, are a gift shop and a bar which serves sandwiches and coffee as well as cold drinks, cocktails, and beer. Rooms in both the main building and the cottages are with bath. Ping-pong, shuffleboard, badminton, and horseshoes are available for guests. A service station and CAA-approved gravel landing strip are directly across the highway from the hotel. Stove Pipe is conveniently located for trips in both central and northern Death Valley, and in the Panamint Mountains. Park Service naturalists regularly conduct evening lecture programs at the hotel once or twice a week during the winter season.

Address inquiries to Stove Pipe Wells Hotel, Death Valley, California.

Wild Rose Station.—Open year round. Located in the Panamint Mountains on the most direct route from Los Angeles. Elevation 3,500 feet. European plan; accommodates ten guests.

All cabins are with bath and are conveniently close to the main building, which serves short orders, coffee, and beer, as well as full-course dinners. Souvenirs, books, film, and staple groceries are available; a service station is operated on the grounds.

Wild Rose was a station on an old freight and stage route and has a long history of serving both Death Valley residents and visitors. It is suitable as headquarters for trips in the Panamint Mountains and in Panamint Valley.

Address inquiries to Wild Rose Station Resort, P.O. Box 4, Trona, California.

Near the Monument

Death Valley Junction.—The Amargosa Hotel, the only overnight accommodation, is open from October to May; service station operated year round. Located east of the Furnace Creek Wash entrance to Death Valley, on State 127. Elevation 2,000 feet.

Hotel rooms are available both with and without bath. A coffee shop and general store are operated in connection with the hotel; also a garage.

Central Death Valley and the Ash Meadows–Pahrump Valley country are easily reached from the Junction.

Address inquires to Fred Harvey Hotels, 530 West 6th Street, Los Angeles 14.

Beatty.—Open year round. Located in Nevada, east of Death Valley, on U.S. 95. Elevation 3,400 feet.

Beatty was established in 1904, concurrently with Rhyolite. It has remained a mine supply center through the ensuing years. Two hotels, half a dozen motels, several cafés, gambling houses, and cocktail lounges serve both the community and travelers. A general store and post office are located on the main street.

The Amargosa Desert and the Daylight Pass area are conveniently close to Beatty.

Panamint Springs.—Usually open year round. Located on State 190 west of the Townes Pass entrance to Death Valley. Elevation 2,000 feet. European plan; accommodates 25 people.

Sleeping cabins with bath are available; some have house-keeping facilities. All have attached garages. Meals and short orders are served throughout the day; dinner is served family style for guests. A gift shop adjoins the dining room and fountain; a service station is adjacent.

Panamint Springs is well located for trips in northern Death Valley and in Panamint Valley.

Address inquiries to Panamint Springs, Darwin, California.

Shoshone.—Open year round. Located east of Death Valley on State 127, the route into the Valley from Baker. Elevation 3,400 feet.

Shoshone has served as a travelers' oasis and mine supply center for half a century. Motel units are available with or without kitchenettes; all with bath. A café and a cocktail lounge are conveniently close to the motel, and a supermarket is across the highway. A service station and garage are operated next to the store. Overnight guests are allowed free use of the community swimming pool.

Shoshone is conveniently located for touring southern Death Valley, and also for the Pahrump Valley–Ash Meadows country.

Address inquiries to Shoshone Motel, Shoshone, California.

Trona and Argus.—Open year round. Adjacent towns west of Death Valley on the approach to the Wildrose Canyon entrance. Elevation 1,600 feet.

The American Chemical and Potash company operates a large plant in Trona, recovering and processing chemicals from near-by Searles Lake. Argus has grown up on the fringe of Trona, which is a company town. The usual small-town accommodations and services are available, including a variety of motels, cafés, cocktail lounges, grocery and general stores, service stations and garages, and a motion picture theater.

Trona and Argus make a convenient stop for Death Valley travelers entering or leaving the Monument through the Panamint Mountains, or for those wishing to explore Panamint Valley.

TRAILERS

A well-shaded trailer court with water and power connections and modern shower, toilet, and laundry facilities is located at Furnace Creek Ranch.

Texas Spring Campgrounds also has trailer space but there are no power or water connections. It is a free public campground maintained by the National Park Service with a 30-day camping limit. Modern rest rooms and piped water are available.

Shoshone, Beatty, Argus, and other communities near the Monument have trailer facilities.

CAMPGROUNDS

Free public campgrounds and campsites are maintained by the National Park Service. Detailed information may be obtained at Park Service headquarters.

The main campground is at Texas Spring in the central Valley; it has a 30-day camping limit. Water, tables, and modern rest rooms are available. Firewood may be purchased at Furnace Creek Ranch.

Mesquite Spring, near Scotty's Castle, is recommended for camping in northern Death Valley. A dozen campsites are situated there in a grove of mesquite trees; tables, water, and pit toilets are available. Firewood must be carried. Midway Well is also designated as a campsite in the northern Valley, but it is not as developed as Mesquite Spring.

In the southern Valley, Eagle Borax Works makes an attractive although undeveloped campsite. Athel trees provide shade and privacy; brackish water is usually obtainable from a pond but it is best to carry drinking and cooking water as well as firewood. Pit toilets are available. Shortys Well and Bennetts Well are also designated as campsites by the National Park Service, but they lack the trees and open water of Eagle Borax Works.

Mahogany Flat, on the crest of the Panamints overlooking the Valley, is a fine hot-weather campsite among the pines. Water is available at Thorndikes, one-half mile below the Flat. Firewood should be carried in; and fires must be carefully watched to prevent forest fire. Wildrose Spring, just below the road Y in lower Wildrose Canyon, offers a small camping space.

Strong gusty winds often come up suddenly in Death Valley and the surrounding mountains, making it advisable to anchor tents well and to lower them to the ground when they are left for the day. A gasoline stove, or some other type of camp stove not requiring wood fuel, is best for cooking purposes. If a fire is desired, wood must be carried; Death Valley plants should never be disturbed.

Leaving a clean campsite is a basic rule. Similarly, the highways should not be littered. Trash cans are placed at parking lots and campgrounds, and trash bags are provided by the National Park Service for convenient use in the car.

Chapter 6

Driving Aids

SERVICES AVAILABLE

The nature of services and facilities both within the Monument and near its borders is subject to change from year to year. Up-to-date information can always be obtained from the National Park Service.

Gas.—Furnace Creek Ranch, Furnace Creek Inn, Death Valley Junction, Shoshone, Beatty, Scotty's Castle, Slim's Place on U.S. 95 at the head of the Grapevine Canyon road, Stove Pipe Wells Hotel, Panamint Springs Resort, Wild Rose Station, Trona.

Repairs and tow car.—Furnace Creek Inn, Death Valley Junction, Shoshone, Beatty, Trona.

Airports.—Paved landing strip, hangar, tie-down, gas and oil at Furnace Creek Ranch; gravel landing strip, tie-down, gas and oil at Stove Pipe Wells Hotel.

Public transportation.—Arrangements must be made in advance for public transportation into Death Valley. Services available vary from year to year; for latest information consult the Park Service or one of the hostelries. Bonanza Airlines usually schedules flights into the Valley. Train and bus travelers may stop over in Las Vegas and charter a car or arrange with the Las Vegas–Tonopah–Reno Stage Line or Tanner Gray Line Tours for transportation into Death Valley. Riddle Tours often runs trips out of Los Angeles and Las Vegas.

Recreation.—Swimming pool, nine-hole all-grass golf course, and stables are located at Furnace Creek Ranch; swimming pool and tennis courts at Furnace Creek Inn.

Meals and snacks.—Furnace Creek Ranch, Furnace Creek Inn, Death Valley Junction, Shoshone, Beatty, Scotty's Castle, Slim's Place, Stove Pipe Wells Hotel, Panamint Springs Resort, Wild Rose Station, Trona.

Groceries.—Furnace Creek Ranch, Death Valley Junction, Shoshone, Beatty, Wild Rose Station (limited selection), Trona.

Information.—National Park Service headquarters, all hostelries, museum at Furnace Creek Ranch, evening programs conducted by Park Service naturalists during the season.

Telephone.—Furnace Creek Ranch, Furnace Creek Inn, National Park Service headquarters. In case of emergency, rangers can handle messages over the National Park Service FM radio.

Post office.—Outgoing mail may be left at any hostelry. The nearest post offices are in Death Valley Junction and Beatty on the east, Trona and Darwin on the west.

Medical service.—A doctor or nurse is usually available at Death Valley Junction; sometimes at Furnace Creek Inn. Trona has the nearest modern, well-equipped hospital. In an emergency, contact the National Park Service.

Desert Driving Suggestions

Highway Travel

Carry water for passengers and car. One gallon per person and five gallons for the radiator per day are conservative allowances in hot weather. Carry more if you are going into the back country.

In summer stay on main roads. They are the only ones maintained and patrolled. State 190, the road through the Panamints, the Scotty's Castle road, and Daylight Pass are considered the main arteries through the Valley.

Gas stations are widely spaced. Watch the gas gauge and know how far it is to the next station.

Carry an accurate map. Know your present location and what lies ahead.

Use second gear on steep up-grades to prevent engine "lug." But when traveling with an up-canyon wind, as is usually the case during the daytime, maintain enough speed to force air through the radiator.

Many grades are actually much steeper than they appear. This is especially true on the alluvial fans.

If the car boils, face it into the wind and leave the engine running. Sprinkle water over the radiator to speed cooling,

NEAR BADWATER

Above: Mushroom Rock

Below: Salt Pool

FURNACE CREEK AREA

Above: Date Garden at Furnace Creek I[

Below: Dump of Borax Mine at Ryan

Dantes View

Zabriskie Point

NEAR SCOTTY'S CASTLE

Above: Death Valley Scotty

Below: Sand Dunes

Above: The Castle

Below: "Little Hebe" Crater, near Ubehebe

IN THE PANAMINTS

Above: Charcoal Kilns

Below: Harrisburg Flat

but do not open the radiator cap until the gauge shows that the water is cooled.

Vapor lock frequently causes trouble, especially when trying to start up again after a long, hot drive. To clear this, cool the fuel pump by wrapping a wet cloth around it and waiting several minutes.

Back-Country Travel

Conditions on back roads change from time to time. Inquire about them before undertaking a back-country trip.

Before leaving on a back-country trip, let a responsible person (preferably a ranger) know your plans. On returning, be sure to check in with the same person, or someone who will notify him.

In remote country, park on a slope so that it will be possible to coast if the car fails to start readily.

On rough roads, a slow speed (often 15 to 25 miles an hour) will save chattering and reduce shock on the car, thereby lessening chances of cut tires and blowouts. It will also prevent violent bouncing, with its attendant loss of clearance. Go up sudden rises gently.

Check on grades before plunging down them; some are difficult to get back up.

To prevent high-centering, run with one set of wheels on the high center and the other wheels along the edge of the road.

If stuck in sand, don't spin the wheels. Let the tires down to 15 pounds and accelerate slowly and evenly. Be sure to pump the tires up again when back on the highway.

On narrow roads, the right of way belongs to the ascending car. Stop at the first place wide enough to pass in order to avoid backing.

A spare tire, jack, pump, tire irons, and repair kit are essentials for a back-country trip.

Two cars traveling together provide a margin of safety in remote country.

If trouble develops it is best to stay with the car. Death Valley holds no particular terror even in summer; there is no reason for alarm if delayed. On a main road, a ranger or another traveler will probably be along within a few hours; in the back country, those who know your plans will be out to help should you fail to return on schedule. Distances are great, and attempting them on foot when unfamiliar with the country only increases the problem. It is best not to walk unless you are used to walking and know where to go. Then, if walking is absolutely necessary, stay along the road and every few miles arrange stones or brush in the road saying "help" and pointing the direction you are heading. In hot weather, walk only during the coolest part of the night (from 10:00 P.M. to sun-up) and stay in the shade during daylight hours. Carry as much water as you can, and drink it rather than conserving it. You will need about a gallon for every 20 miles of summer night-time walking. If you have more than 20 miles to go for help, do not undertake it unless you have water to carry.

Chapter 7

Taking Pictures

CARE OF CAMERA AND FILM

Heat.—Heat deteriorates film, and Death Valley can be hot any month of the year. The best way to protect film from heat when traveling is to carry it in a dust-proof box on the floor of the car, away from the heat of the exhaust pipe. The floor is lower and cooler than the rest of the car, and gets less sun. Using a box that has been painted aluminum or some light color gives additional protection.

Film should not be carried in the glove compartment, on the shelf by the rear window, or in the luggage compartment. Temperatures in these closed-up places sometimes burst a household thermometer and can ignite matches even on days that are not unbearably hot out in the open.

If equipment is to be left closed in the car for any length of time, carry a piece of cloth large enough to put across the windows, covering the sunny side. Special precautions should be taken with exposed film because it is even more sensitive to heat than unexposed. As a rule, film should be sent off for processing as soon as possible.

Dust.—One of the best ways to keep equipment and film free of dust is to carry them in plastic bags that are twisted shut and tightly fastened with rubber bands.

Lenses should be dusted with a camel's hair brush, or blown clean with a syringe. If gentle brushing or blowing fails to remove dust, it is probably because of static electricity. Various antistatic fluids are helpful in breaking the charge. It can also be broken by holding the metal of the lens mount against a waterpipe while brushing, thus grounding it. When changing film, it is advisable to inspect the inside of the camera for dust, and clean it if necessary.

USING THE CAMERA

Coverage.—Points of interest in the Monument range

from broad vistas such as Dantes View and Aguerreberry Point to middle-distance scenes such as Badwater and the old Skidoo gold mill, and to close-ups such as a cactus blossom or a lizard. Death Valley pictures should capture some of this variety.

A successful photograph needs a point of interest and continuity; it needs to be a picture *of* something. This is especially important in taking desert landscapes. The scene's appeal to the eye is heightened by the clean sweep of land, but careful framing is necessary if the film is to record a *picture* instead of a mere fragment of landscape. Pleasing composition is largely subjective. No set of rules guarantees satisfactory results, for good pictures depend on too many variables. Light intensities, color tones, textures, shadows, and strong horizontal, vertical, or curving lines all enter in. A proper blend yields a pleasing composition; a thoughtless combination may not.

A human figure, properly placed, often adds interest to a picture; sometimes a bush or a prominent rock or a bend in the road serves the purpose. People should be pictured doing something appropriate to the scene rather than posing self-consciously. Activities such as picnicking in the Dunes, hiking along the Gower Gulch trail, or drinking from a desert water bag out on the Devils Golfcourse offer good opportunities for pictures.

Lenses.—Cameras without interchangeable lenses usually are equipped with a lens of the focal length normal for the camera's film size, the best lens for a variety of purposes. Fast lenses are seldom needed in Death Valley because light is usually ample. A single-lens camera, possibly equipped with a close-up attachment that slips on, offers inexhaustible picture possibilities in Death Valley. However, the versatility of cameras with interchangeable lens makes them particularly well suited to many subjects.

A moderately long-focus lens (one and one-half to two times normal length) has an advantage over a normal or wide-angle lens in taking scenic pictures. It renders mountains boldly, accentuating their height. Lenses three or more times normal focal length often exclude too much of a scene, but they are valuable for wildlife, and occasionally for scenic effect.

Wide-angle lenses have the effect of flattening mountains. However, in narrow canyons and places where its is inconvenient to get far enough away from the subject for ideal framing, they are very useful. They are also valuable for great depth of focus—although the same effect often can be obtained by increasing the distance between subject and camera.

Film.—In general, color transparencies of any size will satisfactorily record everything in Death Valley from the near by to the distant. However, distant landscapes taken on small-size black-and-white film are frequently disappointing because of poor detail and contrast, except when taken under ideal conditions. Haze is a problem. A scene that will make a pleasing color picture may lack the brilliance and boldness needed for satisfactory monochrome.

All types of film should be changed in the darkest shade available, and even the so-called light-proof cartridges are not always completely safe. Exposed film should be sealed in light-proof, dust-tight containers immediately after removal from the camera.

Exposures.—The light in Death Valley is deceptive. The brightness of the sky affects human reaction to the light; but the usual camera subjects—mountains, rocks, human flesh tones—are comparatively dark. In using a light meter, all light values in the scene should be considered, but care should be taken not to include much sky or light reflected from nearby bright objects. A lens hood is a good precaution against the glare of sky and sand.

Light intensity and quality vary from hour to hour and from subject to subject in Death Valley. There is no "average exposure." However, in general a slight underexposure will render colors pleasingly enriched; and because of the light tolerance of color film emulsions it is usually safer to underexpose than overexpose, if in doubt.

Filters.—The use of filters is largely a matter of individual experience and preference. Their indiscriminate use often results in unwanted effects.

In taking color, a polarizing filter helps minimize Death Valley haze without dulling desert yellows and tans. It is not necessary to set it at full effect unless a dramatic rendition of a scene is wanted. Yellow and red filters will help bring out contrast on black-and-white film, and are consequently valuable for scenics. Even so, broad landscapes taken with small cameras are seldom satisfactory. With them, it is usually better to concentrate on middle-distance and close-up shots.

Light.—Early and late lights are the best times for taking Death Valley pictures. Sunrise and sunset are good for dramatic shots, but for most purposes a few hours after sunrise and a few hours before sunset are the best times. The molding effect of the light is excellent at those times, and shadows lend character and depth to pictures. Midday light is flat but is best for many deep canyons, and is fine for close-ups.

If time can be scheduled flexibly, photographic plans should depend somewhat on the weather. A particularly hazy day or one with winds stirring up dust is a poor one for landscapes, but can prove rewarding for canyons and middle-distance points of interest. Overcast days can be similarly used. The best time for scenics is immediately after a rain. The atmosphere is clear then and the desert tones rich.

Pictures can be taken a little earlier in the morning on the west side of the Valley than on the east, and later into the afternoon along the Funeral and Black Mountains than in the Panamints. The sand dunes are equally good in first-light or last, but sundown has the advantage of lengthening shadows, while at sunrise it is hard to anticipate where shadows will fall, and once cast they become shorter and weaker.

Chapter 8

Sights on the Main Roads

The choice of what to see is largely a matter of time—time of day as well as number of hours. For example, Dantes View is best in the morning; Aguerreberry Point in the afternoon. Weather can also influence the question of which trips to take. On a hot day, the high country of Harrisburg Flat and upper Wildrose, the Black Mountains, or the Daylight Pass area will be particularly enjoyable. On a chilly day a tour of the Valley floor is more in order: a loop of the Bad-water and West Side roads, or a drive to the northern Valley and Scotty's Castle. Occasionally the wind raises dust in the mountains and Valley, blotting out the distances. On such days the protection of canyons is welcome, or time may be well spent in the museum at Furnace Creek Ranch.

ON THE WAY TO BADWATER

Places.—Past FAULT SCARP; up GOLDEN CANYON and back to the highway; on to MUSHROOM ROCK; over to the SALT POOLS and PINNACLES; and south to BADWATER.

Possible side trips.—NATURAL BRIDGE, ARTISTS DRIVE.

Possible loop trip.—On south from BADWATER and back to the central Valley either by way of the unpaved WEST SIDE road or up JUBILEE and SALSBURY PASSES, then to State 190 by way of SHOSHONE or through the unpaved GREEN-WATER cutoff.

Roads.—The main road is paved but the side roads are not, except for part of Artists Drive. However, the dirt roads are graded and maintained and are readily passable.

Map.—Page 43.

Suggested time.—Three or four hours, preferably in the afternoon for best light in the canyons; longer if plans include a stroll in Golden Canyon, or at Natural Bridge.

41

Picture ideas.—The view out the mouth of GOLDEN CAN-
YON, best in midday light; MUSHROOM ROCK taken to emphasize the slender stem; the SALT PINNACLES in strong, slanting
light; BADWATER very early in the morning, reflecting Telescope Peak; ARTISTS PALETTE, midway through ARTISTS
DRIVE, for color pictures.

Tour.—The FAULT SCARP, along the foot of the Black
Mountains, a mile south of Furnace Creek Inn, was formed
by block faulting, one of the prime earth forces geologically
responsible for Death Valley. It is a two- to six-foot bank
marking an abrupt lowering of the Valley floor that probably
occurred during the earthquake period of 1872.

GOLDEN CANYON threads among the mud hills a mile farther south. The red clay at its entrance was called *dumbisha*
by the Indians, who used it for face paint. They referred to
the whole central Valley as Dumbisha, meaning literally "rock
face paint," but usually poetically mistranslated "ground
afire." Except for the "face paint" the clays of the canyon
are gold-colored, particularly in late afternoon light. The
passageway is narrow; the walls sheer.

At the end of the road (one and one-half miles) an old
trail strikes off northeastward to a natural amphitheater
called RED CATHEDRAL. It is about a half-hour hike. A
quarter-mile down-canyon from the parking area another trail
heads up GOWER GULCH to the base of MANLY BEACON, a
pinnacle of golden clay.

Freak cooling of molten rock originally shaped MUSH-
ROOM ROCK, south of Golden Canyon, and wind and salt have
sculptured it further. The wind blasts it with sand and salt,
which lodge in its pores. When it rains, the salt dissolves;
then recrystallizes as it drys, flaking off tiny bits of stone.

The spur road to the SALT POOLS and PINNACLES is six
miles south of Mushroom Rock. The Pinnacles are of rock
salt which analyzes almost pure sodium chloride, common
table salt, only lightly mixed with soil washed and blown
from surrounding country. Formed into knife-edged spires
and ridges one to two feet high, they "grow" by capillary
action. Salt dissolved in water is drawn up and left to crystallize as the water evaporates, thus adding slowly and steadily
to the pinnacles until an occasional deluge wears them away,
whereupon the process starts over again.

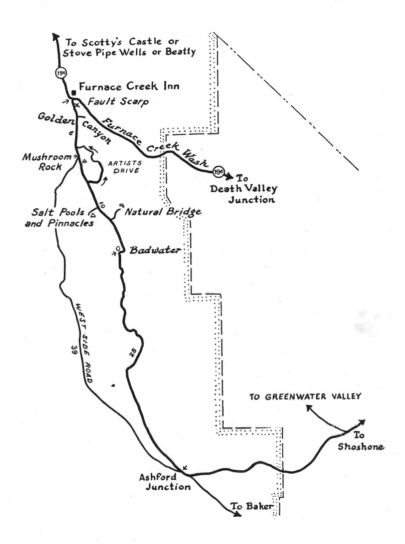

The Salt Pools were kept open years ago by blasting holes in the salt. They filled with water so supersaturated with salt that it was possible to hear a continual tinkling sound as it crystallized from the evaporating water. The pools are seldom found nowadays.

Just north of Badwater is an immense rounded cliff called the TURTLEBACK FAULT SCARP. It is somewhat eroded but otherwise very smooth, making it easy to visualize a great block of the earth's crust having cracked and slipped along its face.

The stagnant pool of BADWATER is the ultimate sink for the Amargosa River which winds south through the Amargosa Desert and then turns north into Death Valley. The name "Badwater" comes from a surveyor's candid notation on an early map. Water in the lower elevations is often "bad" because of minerals leached into it, but not poisonous. However, early-day travelers sometimes got sick from it because of Glauber's and Epsom salts which are often present. Badwater, — 279 feet, was believed the lowest point in the Western Hemisphere until 1951 when the Geological Survey found two spots a few miles northwest that are each three feet lower. This hemispheric low of — 282 feet is exceeded on only two continents: in Africa where the Qattara Depression is 440 feet below sea level, and in Asia where the Dead Sea is — 1,290 feet.

A half-hour's walk west of Badwater leads among mud "saucers," six feet across, rimmed by salt.

Side trips.—NATURAL BRIDGE: north of Badwater; the road up the fan is steeper than it seems and cars sometimes overheat.

The parking area is reached soon after entering a mud-walled canyon, about two miles up the fan. A good view of the bridge is about one-tenth of a mile up-canyon; and one-tenth of a mile farther the bridge itself arches 50 feet overhead. About 150 feet beyond the bridge, there is a chute marking where cloudburst runoff has spilled over the canyon rim and cut the wall. Half a dozen polished "spillways" around the next bend mark a grotto cut 75 feet into the canyon wall by water. The "benches" along the canyon sides indicate former levels of the wash.

ARTISTS DRIVE: One-way drive; enter from the south. The road is narrow with occasional sharp curves and steep grades.

Views of the salt flats and the southern sweep of the Valley may be had by looking back from time to time while climbing the fan. Artists Palette, five miles from the highway, is a jumble of colored muds. Iron oxides are responsible for the red tones, manganese oxides for the green.

THE FURNACE CREEK AREA

Places.—HARMONY BORAX WORKS and MUSTARD CANYON, up FURNACE CREEK WASH, to ZABRISKIE POINT and back to the highway, through 20-MULE TEAM CANYON, and on to DANTES VIEW.

Possible side trips.—RYAN, GREENWATER.

Possible loop trip.—Through GREENWATER VALLEY after leaving DANTES VIEW and back into Death Valley by SALSBURY and JUBILEE PASSES, then north along either the BADWATER highway or the graded road on the WEST SIDE.

Roads.—Paved except for the side trip to Greenwater. The last grade up to Dantes View is steep but readily passable, and there is level parking and turning space at the top.

Map.—Page 46.

Suggested time.—Three or four hours, preferably in the morning; longer for looking around the ghost towns. Dantes View is best when the sun is low on the eastern horizon.

Picture ideas.—The ruins of HARMONY BORAX WORKS with its crumbling adobe walls framing the Funeral Mountains; ZABRISKIE POINT's eroded mud hills, in strongly slanting light (early morning or late afternoon); the road winding through bare hills in 20-MULE TEAM CANYON; Death Valley and Nevada panoramas from DANTES VIEW; the old schoolhouse at RYAN, and the bunkhouses.

Tour.—HARMONY BORAX WORKS, a mile north of Furnace Creek, was a crude refinery started in 1882, and operated for five years, employing about 40 men. A fluffy-looking borax called ulexite ("cottonball") was hauled in from the marsh near by, heated in vats with water and carbonate, and then crystallized on iron rods suspended in the solution. After drying, the borax was loaded in wagons and freighted by 20-mule teams to the railroad at Mojave, a 165-mile trip requiring about ten overnight camps, nearly half of which were waterless.

Beyond the adobe walls, which are the ruins of office

buildings, the road winds through Mustard Canyon. It is a short drive (half a mile) worth taking for its close-up view of the badlands formation common in central Death Valley.

Furnace Creek Wash is reached by turning south after leaving Mustard Canyon. Up the wash, just beyond the Inn gas station, there is a small area of strangely eroded cliffs and "islands" of sun-hardened mud. Warm Springs, where the forty-niners quenched their thirst after waterless days on the Amargosa Desert, is a short way beyond. A flume now carries the water to the Inn and Ranch where it is used for domestic purposes, irrigation, and power generation.

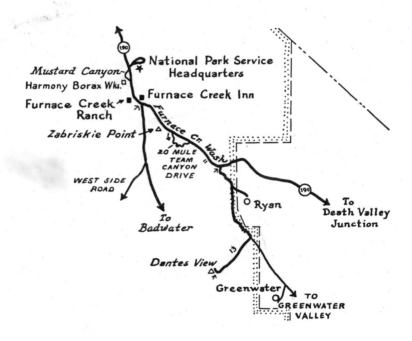

Three miles beyond the Inn, a paved road one-quarter mile long turns off to Zabriskie Point, named for Christian Brevoort Zabriskie who followed "Borax" Smith as head of the early-day borax company. Ancient lake beds, now up-ended into a mass of weathered yellow mudhills, spread below the parking area. The sharp, delicately banded mud peak on the Valley side is Manly Beacon.

A mile farther, State 190 passes the entrance of 20-Mule Team Canyon where a one-way graded road, four and a half miles long, climbs and dips among the rounded hills. The building now housing displays at the Ranch stood halfway through the drive until 1952. It is said to be the first frame house in Death Valley, built as a boarding house for borax miners and teamsters. The 20-mule teams, commemorated in the naming of this canyon, never freighted through it—their route from Harmony Borax Works was south through the Valley and out over Wingate Pass. However, smaller teams freighted through the canyon.

The Valley lies over a mile below DANTES VIEW. Badwater is too near the base of the mountains to be seen, but the two points northwest of it that are the actual hemispheric lows (−282 feet) are visible, although no particular landmark identifies them. The High Sierra shows far to the west on a clear day. In the Valley, directly across from Dantes View, Eagle Borax Works and Bennetts Well appear as dark green spots. Telescope Peak, high point in the Panamints, is over a mile higher than Dantes View.

Side trips.—RYAN: Six borax mines were worked at Ryan: the upper and lower Biddies, the Louise, Oakley, Grand View, and Widow. The mines were served by a two-foot baby-gauge railroad, and were connected with Tonopah and Tidewater rails by a 15-mile narrow-gauge road.

Ryan was active from 1914 to 1928. It was abandoned in favor of a more profitable operation near Mojave. Worn carpeting and Roaring Twenties furniture still grace the family homes; awnings are neatly rolled on the bunkhouse screen porches; the bell tops the little school; inside the recreation hall the stage curtain's sailing ship breasts the painted waves, and player-piano rolls lie where they were last used. The hall was once the Catholic Church of Rhyolite, a gold camp whose day was finished before Ryan's began. Such salvaging of buildings and materials is a common desert practice. New camps are built from dead camps.

Occasionally Ryan's Death Valley View Hotel is opened to accommodate overflow crowds from the Ranch and Inn, and sometimes the bunkhouses are used by touring school groups.

GREENWATER: Reached by a graded dirt road; the side roads off of it are not maintained but usually are in good condition. (See also pages 65 to 67.)

Greenwater was a turn-of-the-century copper camp. More than a thousand people settled it within a month after a copper strike in 1905. Soon the town had a bank, a post office, telephones, a men's magazine called *The Chuckwalla*—everything except paying ore.

Several roads turn up to the sites of Greenwater and to Furnace, another copper camp. The main road is about eight miles from the pavement. Little remains of the towns except a litter of beer bottles, rusted stoves, parts of Model T's, an occasional houseless basement, and several vertical shafts, one of them 1,600 feet deep.

NEAR SCOTTY'S CASTLE

Places.—To SCOTTY'S CASTLE, and on to UBEHEBE CRATER.

Possible side trips.—SAND DUNES, DEVILS CORNFIELD, RHYOLITE, the RACETRACK for a back-country trip.

Roads.—Paved except for the side trip to the Dunes. The Racetrack road is often rough.

Map.—Page 49.

Suggested time.—Four or five hours; longer if the side trips are to be included. Early morning or late afternoon is best for the Dunes and the Cornfield. During the travel season tours are conducted through the Castle hourly, seven days a week.

Picture ideas. — The CASTLE grounds from the clock tower and from the hill across the highway; the Original Castle, a shack behind the Guest House; Scotty's Grave atop the hill; UBEHEBE CRATER from the point on the rim, south of the parking area; contours and ripple patterns in the DUNES accentuated by slanting light; the DEVILS CORNFIELD, also best in slanting light; the Bottle House at RHYOLITE and the ruined buildings along Golden Street.

Tour.—The Scotty's Castle road branches off State 190 about 18 miles north of Furnace Creek. Dips are frequent, and accidents have occurred when drivers have suddenly met another car formerly hidden in a dip.

The dirt road turning left two miles after leaving State 190 runs a mile west to STOVEPIPE WELL. (The hotel of the same name is nearly ten miles southwest, on the highway.) The well was so named because years ago a prospector thrust a length of stovepipe in the sand to keep the waterhole open. During the Rhyolite and Skidoo days Stovepipe Well was an important source of water on the main route across the Valley, and a roadhouse was operated there. Little is left of the roadhouse now, and the old stovepipe is replaced by a pump. A grave marked with the name Val Nolan is near by. All that is known of him is recorded on his headboard: "Died about Aug. 6, 1931. Buried Nov. 6, 1931. Victim of the elements."

MESQUITE SPRING, an old Indian campsite, is a mile and a half off the pavement just beyond the Grapevine Ranger Station. The warm spring flows continuously; but its water, like that of most desert streams, does not go far before it sinks into the sand. The Park Service has built tables and simple rock fireplaces under the trees. Pit toilets are down the wash from the spring.

The entrance to SCOTTY'S CASTLE is three miles up-canyon

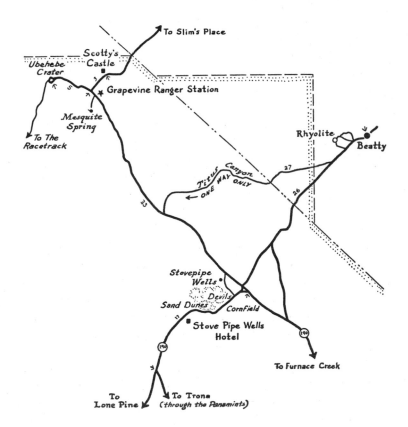

from the junction with the Ubehebe road. Both Walter Scott and A. M. Johnson, his financial backer, are dead. Scotty, who died in January 1954 at the age of 81, is buried atop a hill behind "the shack," as he loved to call the sumptuous mansion.

During Scotty's lifetime, rumors of a gold mine surrounded his every move, and there really was one—Johnson's pockets! Johnson was a Chicago insurance millionaire who took a fancy to the flamboyant desert rat and former Wild West Show trick rider. The two teamed up and, with Johnson's money and Scotty's enthusiasm, built the Castle as a combination home, joke, self-memorial, and monument to craftsmanship.

It was begun in 1924 and supposedly cost over two million dollars, although the work is not yet completed—and probably never will be. A 185-foot swimming pool is one of the more conspicuously unfinished touches of grandeur. There would have been plenty of water for it. Grapevine Spring supplies 600 gallons a minute: enough for domestic use, and to generate electricity, fill a wishing well in the courtyard, and splash over an elaborate jasper fountain into a goldfish pool in the two-story living room.

The Castle is not administered by the National Park Service. Since Johnson's death in 1948 it has been operated by a Los Angeles charitable foundation which conducts tours through the buildings for a nominal fee. Furnishings are elaborate, many of them imported antiques and others made on the premises, carefully styled after Old World art treasures.

UBEHEBE CRATER, an explosion crater, is five miles beyond the turn-off to the Castle. It is the most prominent and colorful of a group of more than half a dozen craters. A short hike south from the high point on Ubehebe's rim leads to a nearly perfect cone located inside a worn-down crater.

Ubehebe measures half a mile across at the top and is 800 feet deep. The Indians say that it used to be a big basket; however their name, "Ubehebe," does not mean "basket-in-the-rock" as it has often been translated. Instead the area was referred to as Ubehebe because a woman of that name lived near by. The crater itself was called Duh-vee'tah Wah'sah, "Duhveetah's Carrying Basket."

Side trips.—SAND DUNES: The dirt road south of Stovepipe Wells leads to the edge of the Dunes. There is a good parking place a mile and a half below the well, at the Easter Bowl where annual sunrise services are held.

The dunes of bare sand cover about 14 square miles, and mesquite-sand hummocks cover a much larger area. Wind ripples the surface of the sand and often stirs up blinding sand storms, but eddies keep the dunes in place. Their main contours are unchanged from year to year, with the highest dune remaining in about the same location.

DEVILS CORNFIELD: The "corn shocks" along State 190 are arrowweed plants, so named because the Indians made arrow shafts from the stems. On hot days the salt marsh of the Cornfield acts as a giant evaporative cooler, dropping the air temperature as its moisture evaporates.

RHYOLITE: The ruins of Rhyolite, a town that mined three million dollars worth of gold, lie 25 miles from the Valley floor, beyond Daylight Pass. A spectacular back-country trip can be combined with a visit to Rhyolite by driving to Chloride City and then through Titus Canyon. Current road conditions should be checked first; see pages 67 to 70.

Rhyolite was one of Nevada's more flourishing cities from 1905 to 1908. The ruins of the school, bank building, doctor's office, and store still line Golden Street. The old jailhouse is east of Golden; the Las Vegas and Tonopah Railroad depot is on a side street. A few adobe walls and some stone foundations remain, but long gone are the frame and tent houses that once sheltered and served Rhyolite's 5,000 to 10,000 citizens—the population depending on how many suburbs are included. An unusual house is one built of 51,000 quart beer bottles. It is open to visitors.

Bullfrog, site of the strike responsible for Rhyolite, is west of the main town. The graveyard is a mile south of the Bottle House. The hill toward Beatty is cut by the Montgomery-Shoshone Mine, famous for its Glory Hole, where gold ore was quarried. The dumps of the Tramp Mine are prominent on the hill west of town. The Montgomery had an 18-stamp mill to crush the ore; the Tramp, a 12-stamp mill.

THE RACETRACK: The road turns off beyond Ubehebe Crater; a check should be made on road conditions. See page 63 for details of the trip.

51

IN THE PANAMINTS

Places. — Through EMIGRANT CANYON, past a FAULT and JOURNIGANS MILL to SKIDOO, then over to AGUERRE-BERRY POINT.

Possible side trips.—GROTTO and MOSAIC CANYONS, CHARCOAL KILNS, MAHOGANY FLAT.

Roads.—Main road paved; graded dirt roads to Skidoo and Aguerreberry Point. The road to the Kilns is unpaved most of the way and is steep just before reaching Mahogany Flat.

Map.—Page 53.

Suggested time.—Three or four hours; longer if the side trips are to be included. Aguerreberry Point is best in after-noon light.

Picture ideas.—The old buildings at SKIDOO with the High Sierra in the background; the Million Dollar Portal (mouth of a mine that was a rich producer), taken with flash equipment; the view from AGUERREBERRY POINT, best in the afternoon; CHARCOAL KILNS, preferably in slanting light; the trees and views at MAHOGANY FLAT.

Tour.—The road into the Panamints branches south from State 190 at the Emigrant Ranger Station. Nine-tenths of a mile beyond the turn there appears to be a gentle down-grade, but an unbraked car will not roll on it. The illusion of the grade is created by the road crossing a remnant of an old fan which has been left an "island" by new drainage channels. The downward slope of the main wash makes this stretch of road seem to slant, but actually it is level.

The entrance of EMIGRANT CANYON, a mile farther on, has striking erosion patterns in the brown cliffs on each side of the road. The canyon walls are fanglomerate—ancient alluvial fan material hardened to rock. A FAULT may be seen by looking back to the right just after passing a cliff with a chain of eight-foot caves on its face. A gray-layer that has been offset about 20 feet emphasizes the slippage, which is an excellent example of block faulting.

JOURNIGANS MILL, a gold mill and camp west of the high-way, intermittently mills ore from Tucki Mountain mines.

The SKIDOO road turns left across the edge of Harrisburg Flat about three miles farther on. The scar of the old pipeline across the desert is noticeable two miles after making the turn, running at right angles to the road.

During Skidoo's early days drinking water was hauled from Emigrant Spring, 15 miles away, and sold for ten cents a gallon; but a better source was needed before a mill could

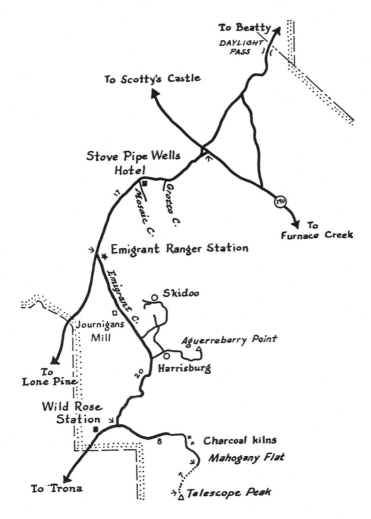

operate. Birch Spring, high on Telescope Peak, was decided upon as the best source and an eight-inch pipeline was put in —a project that took 18 months. According to one story, the name of the then-flourishing camp was taken from the pipeline. It was 23 miles to the spring; and "23 Skidoo" was the smart saying of the day. Another version of the naming discredits the pipeline mileage and mentions that 23 men founded the town. Still another story says that originally there were 23 mine claims.

The Skidoo road climbs steadily, frequently offering views of Death Valley; Mt. Charleston is the snowy peak in the distance, east of the Valley. Furnace Creek Wash shows plainly as the wide pass between the Funeral Mountains and the Black Mountains. Big Dune, in the Amargosa Desert, rises beyond the northern Funerals.

After two and a half miles of climbing, the road turns west and heads across a broad stretch of level land. The Skidoo graveyard is off the road to the left, a mile after starting across the level. The remaining buildings of Skidoo, once a town of 700, are visible nearly a mile farther on. The old office building stands on the brow of a hill, with the Cottonwood Mountains rearing up beyond and the Sierra ultimately topping the intervening ranges. Mines are numerous, and many are worked intermittently. The tunnel directly across from the office is the Million Dollar Portal, where a single stope, or side tunnel, yielded a million dollars' worth of gold. A vertical shaft is atop the hill. The assay building and 15-stamp mill are in the canyon behind the office. A section of the Birch Spring pipeline is still in place in the old mill. Skidoo ore was rich, making the town unique in Death Valley mining annals as having been profitable. Three million dollars were poured into the ground and six million taken out.

The three-and-a-half-mile road connecting the Skidoo road and the AGUERREBERRY POINT road is readily passable and shorter than going back to the pavement. In the early 1900's a herd of goats, Skidoo's meat supply, grazed on the flat the road now crosses. Leaks in the Skidoo pipeline provided water, and at that time there was grass as well as sagebrush and saltbush.

HARRISBURG doubtless shared the goat meat. It was a tent city that grew up around a gold strike made by Shorty Harris and Pete Aguerreberry a few days before the Skidoo strike. In fact, it was while lost en route to Harrisburg that Harry Ramsey and One Eye Thompson found the ore outcropping that started the Skidoo rush. Harrisburg is now only a scar on the desert. Little more than the mine remains, occasionally operated by Pete Aguerreberry's descendants.

Pete, a Basque sheepherder who came to this country to herd sheep but was struck with gold fever, laid out the first road to Aguerreberry Point, a viewpoint four miles beyond the Harrisburg Mine. There are two fairly steep, narrow canyons on the road but they are each only a half-mile long and offer no difficulties.

The building at the end of the road is a Park Service FM radio relay station. A short trail north of it leads to the best viewpoint. The panorama of the Valley stretches from Mormon Point, south of Badwater, to the Daylight Pass area. The hills behind the Inn seem insignificant from the height of Aguerreberry Point, and the Ranch looks like a mere square of black connected with the Inn by the irrigation ditch.

Side trips.—GROTTO CANYON and MOSAIC CANYON: These two canyons cut into Tucki Mountain near Stove Pipe Wells Hotel. The Grotto Canyon road turns from State 190 two and a half miles east of the hotel; the Mosaic Canyon turn is one-tenth of a mile south of the hotel. Mosaic is probably the better choice if time only permits walking into one of the two canyons.

An unusual breccia, or natural mosaic, on the lower walls gives Mosaic Canyon its name. In 1951 a cloudburst brought mud down the canyon, covering the mosaic pattern, but later rains have washed it clean. Around the first bend is a great slab of low-grade marble, smoothed and sculptured by the streams that occasionally rush down the canyon.

The first chamber of Grotto Canyon is reached after a half-mile walk up the wash from the road's end. A succession of similar water-carved grottoes with canyon walls nearly touching overhead follow close on one another. The way is difficult, because of increasingly high dry-waterfalls that have to be scaled. In less than a mile there is an amphitheater with sheer walls about 50 feet high.

CHARCOAL KILNS: In the 1860's the pinyon pines in upper Wildrose Canyon were the nearest source of fuel for the smelter at the Modoc Mines, owned by George Hearst, father of the late publisher William Randolph Hearst. Accordingly, the Kilns were built to make charcoal, which was then packed on mules 25 miles across Panamint Valley to the smelter. The Kilns were designed by Swiss engineers, built by Chinese laborers, and stoked by Death Valley Indians.

All ten Kilns still stand. They are 30 feet across and look like enormous beehives made of stone. A small lime kiln is up the hill from them. They are easily reached by the dirt road into upper Wildrose Canyon. The grade is steeper than it looks; driving in low gear may be advisable part of the way.

MAHOGANY FLAT: The road becomes steeper beyond the Kilns; it climbs past Thorndike's place, the former home of a man prominent in Death Valley mining history, and comes out at a saddle on the crest of the range. Snow sometimes blocks the road in winter.

The road north from the parking area leads to an undeveloped picnic and camp area. Water is not available at the Flat but may be obtained at Thorndike's. The Telescope Peak trail south of the parking area is worth walking along for at least half a mile, to the first bench, so as to see the sweep of Death Valley framed by pine trees. It is seven miles to the summit. Water should be carried.

Chapter *9*

The Back Country by Car

Much of Death Valley's back country is accessible over dirt roads built for mining use and still passable although in most cases no longer regularly used or maintained. Their conditions vary from time to time, and additional roads occasionally are scraped as new mines open. Current road information may be obtained at National Park Service headquarters.

THE WEST SIDE ROAD

Places.—Across the DEVILS GOLFCOURSE, along the WEST SIDE SPRINGS and WELLS, past the HANAUPAH FAULT SCARP and the HARRIS-DAYTON GRAVES to EAGLE BORAX WORKS.

Possible side trips.—BUTTE VALLEY, TRAIL CANYON.

Possible loop trip.—South past SHORELINE BUTTE, on to ASHFORD JUNCTION, and back up the BADWATER road.

Road.—Graded and maintained; seldom patrolled. The West Side road is easy to drive, but often rough. The Trail Canyon and Butte Valley roads sometimes are in poor condition.

Map.—Page 58.

Suggested time.—Two or three hours; longer if Trail Canyon is included; all day with the side trip to Butte Valley or for the loop trip.

Picture ideas.—The churned salt and mud in the DEVILS GOLFCOURSE, best in strongly slanting light; the pond and marsh at EAGLE BORAX WORKS with the snowy Panamints as background; waterbirds at the Eagle Borax pond.

Tour.—The trip down the West Side of the Valley floor is one of the easiest back-country drives. The road turns off the Badwater highway six miles south of the Inn.

A mile and a half beyond the turn-off the road edges into the salt of the DEVILS GOLFCOURSE—foot-high pinnacles lightly overlaid with mud. An iron casing, used during World War I to drill for potash, lies west of the road a half mile after entering the Devils Golfcourse. The drill went through 1,250 feet of salt and clay, but no potash was found.

TULE SPRING is off the road to the left about five miles beyond the Devils Golfcourse. This is probably where the Bennett-Arcane party camped in 1849 while they waited for John Rogers and William Manly to find a way out of Death

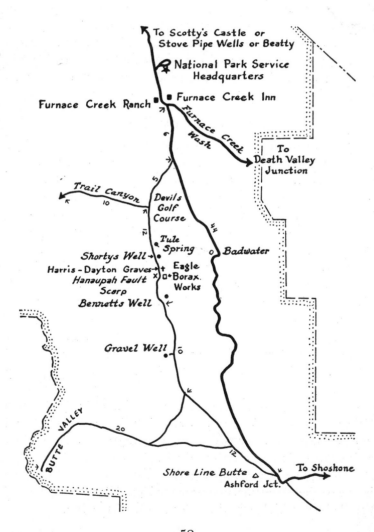

BUTTE VALLEY

Above: Striped Butte

Below: Prospector's Cabin

RACETRACK

RHYOLITE

Left: Moving Rocks

Above: Racetrack Playa

Below: General Store

Ghost Town of Rhyolite

TITUS CANYON   Lead Mine

Near the Mouth of the Canyon

CHLORIDE CITY

Above: Remains of the Town

Below: West of Chloride City

Valley to the settlements. References in Manly's book, *Death Valley in '49*, seem to indicate this watering hole. However the present-day Indians say that the "hairy-faced ones" stayed at Toah Poize (Bennetts Well), keeping the Shoshones out of a winter camp they prized above all others because of the protection of its mesquite.

Off the road to the right is a 10- to 30-foot embankment paralleling the Panamints: the HANAUPAH FAULT SCARP. It is the result of a slip in the earth's crust that is thought to have taken place late in the nineteenth century.

The HARRIS-DAYTON GRAVES are a mile and a half farther south. Jim Dayton was a caretaker at Furnace Creek Ranch who died at the age of 62 while on a summer trip out of the Valley for supplies, in 1899. When he failed to return on schedule, Dolph Nevares and Frank Tilton set out to look for him. They found his body lying under a mesquite, his dog on guard beside it. As they dug a grave Tilton muttered, "Jimmy, you lived in the heat and died in the heat, and now I suppose you've gone to hell."

Shorty Harris' funeral also had an unorthodox touch when mourners and a CCC chaplain gathered to carry out his last wish in 1934. He was a friend of Dayton's and had requested, "Bury me beside Jim Dayton in the Valley we love. Above me write: 'Here lies Shorty Harris, a single-blanket jackass prospector.' "

The grave had been dug by two old friends who evidently worked with Shorty's size in mind, rather than the standard dimensions of a coffin. When the service was read the casket did not fit the grave, and there was a delay while the diggers enlarged the grave. Mourners grew chilled as the sun dropped behind the Panamints and one called out, "Oh, bend the s.o.b. in the middle and plant him. Let's get it over with." The coffin was consequently tilted into the still-too-small grave and they "got it over with."

EAGLE BORAX WORKS, the first borax plant in Death Valley, is a half-mile off the road south of the Harris-Dayton Graves. Isidore Daunet found the borax marsh when he left the played-out camp of Panamint in 1875, but he gave it no thought until six years later when the excitement of Aaron Winters' borax discovery spread across the desert. Daunet went back to the marsh and located 260 acres, then bought an iron vat and six 1,000-gallon pans in Daggett and freighted them the 140 miles into Death Valley. Fifty men set to work bringing in borax for refining, but it proved impure. The best price they could get was eight cents a pound, only about a quarter of the usual price for borax. Operations ceased after less than 150 pounds had been produced.

The vat remains in place and the semicircular marks of the pans still show. Borax that was scraped up by the Eagle Borax men is still mounded on the marsh beyond the athel grove, east of the pond. In years when the pond is extensive, various waterbirds can usually be seen in the marsh.

Side trips.—BUTTE VALLEY: (See below.)

TRAIL CANYON: Indians used Trail Canyon each year in traveling from winter camp on the Valley floor to summer camp among the pinyons of upper Wildrose. Mines operate in all three forks from time to time. Tungsten has been produced in quantity. In 1955 a road was blasted up the northern fork of Trail Canyon to connect with the Aguerreberry Point road, thus facilitating the shipment of ore.

Mine buildings and equipment should not be disturbed; periodic use is common even at camps that look long abandoned.

BUTTE VALLEY

Places.—Up WARM SPRINGS CANYON, into BUTTE VALLEY, past STRIPED BUTTE, on to ANVIL SPRING.

Road.—Graded as far as Warm Springs Talc Mine; not regularly maintained beyond that point but usually readily passable.

Map.—Page 61.

Suggested time.—All day.

Picture ideas.—The WARM SPRINGS oasis; the western face of STRIPED BUTTE.

Tour.—The WARM SPRINGS CANYON road turns off the West Side road 13 miles south of Eagle Borax Works. The extreme right-hand road at the junction runs to the Queen of Sheba Mine, the metal buildings visible at the foot of the Panamints. The remains of Sheba's pumphouse are east of the main road.

An increasingly grand view of the Valley may be had by looking back from time to time while climbing the fan to the canyon mouth. The height and length of the alluvial fans sweeping from the ramparts of the Panamints to the salt flats are particularly impressive. A draw two and a half miles after turning off the West Side road gives a good idea of the actual size of the fans' drainage channels. They look like mere traceries from a distance, such as at Dantes View, but the main wash in this draw is from 50 to 75 feet deep.

The mouth of Warm Springs Canyon is six miles up the fan. The tracks veering south from the main road lead to a mine and also to a junction with the West Side road. The first talc dump is passed soon after entering the Canyon. The mines produce thousands of tons a month. One vein is as

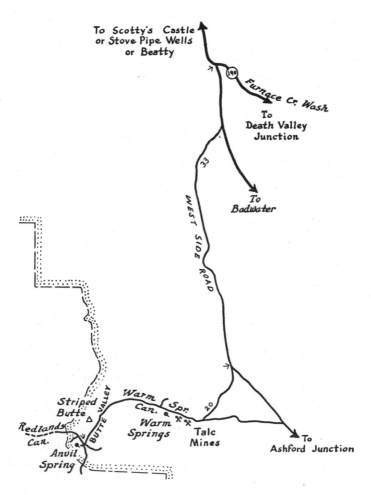

61

much as 25 feet thick, runs at least 3,800 feet, and has been penetrated over 1,000 feet. Most of it is steatite, the purest talc, used in over a hundred industries. For 19 years, while the claims were being developed, one of the owners supported the work with poker winnings, estimated at $40,000.

Enormous fig trees set out in the 1890's, athels, and oleander bushes surround the mine cookhouse and bunkhouses, south of the road. Beyond the camp the road winds up the wash a couple of miles and then makes a fork—the first of many forks, most of which ends at mines.

BUTTE VALLEY lies three miles farther, at an elevation of 4,500 feet. It is reached by taking the left-hand road at the fork, and keeping left again out of the canyon. STRIPED BUTTE is visible soon after entering Butte Valley—a low, sharp, dark peak rising from the Valley floor. Its calico-colored bands, noticeable farther on, indicate its sedimentary origin. The surrounding country is granite, a nonsedimentary rock, making the butte geologically unique.

ANVIL SPRING, on a spur road, has a lone cottonwood tree and a stone cabin known locally as the "Geologist's Shack." The spring is often trampled by wild burros. Roads go in all directions near the spring. Most are passable in a car if driven slowly.

The road north of Anvil Spring affords the best view of Striped Butte. Yellow and almost-red strata mingle with the blacks, grays, and browns. A sign marks the road into Redlands Canyon, believed by some to be the way the Bennett-Arcane party left Death Valley in 1849. It is passable in a jeep for about seven miles.

By keeping left at a jumble of huge boulders, it is possible to drive to a three-stamp gold mill, set in a granite amphitheater. It was built and operated about 1898 by Carl Mengel, a Death Valley old-timer. He purchased the equipment in Los Angeles and hauled it up Goler Wash by mule team. The timbers had been used in the construction of the old Third Street tunnel in Los Angeles.

By keeping right where the tracks turn to the old mill, it is possible to wind among granite boulders to a prospector's "house" walled-up beneath an overhanging boulder the size of a railroad car. A stolen Wells Fargo safe was once found blasted open in "Outlaw Cave," uphill from the rock house.

THE RACETRACK

Places.—The RACETRACK.

Possible side trips.—HIDDEN VALLEY, ASBESTOS MINE, GOLDBELT.

Roads.—Unpaved and irregularly maintained. Sometimes rough but no bad grades except for the side trips.

Map.—Page 64.

Suggested time.—From central Death Valley to the Racetrack and back requires a minimum of five to six hours, and preferably all day, with an early start and a late return to include the side trips.

Picture ideas.—The Joshua trees along the road; the MOVING ROCKS at the RACETRACK.

Tour.—From UBEHEBE CRATER to the RACETRACK is 26 miles. (See page 50 for Ubehebe Crater.) Edging out of the black cinder area, the road between the Cottonwood and Last Chance ranges passes through one of the best cactus gardens in Death Valley. Cottontop, cholla, beavertail, and hedgehog are profuse. Farther on, stunted Joshua trees, members of the lily family, grow on Tin Mountain up to the pinyon-juniper belt.

A road fork locally known as Teakettle Junction is reached about 20 miles after turning onto the Racetrack road. For years a teakettle at the base of a creosote bush was the only sign distinguishing this intersection from any other, a common system of marking in the desert. Directions to "Turn right at the teakettle and then keep left till you come to the old rocking chair" are typical of the desert. Sometimes graves are similarly used: "Go south 12 miles, then turn east at Tim Ryan."

At Teakettle Junction, the right fork leads to the Racetrack, a playa, or dry lake bed, at the southern end of a 3,700-foot valley. Indians supposedly raced horses on the smooth oval of the dry lake, using the "island" that rises near its northern shore as a grandstand.

The MOVING ROCKS range from walnut size to that of an apple box. The largest rocks, five blocks of limestone weighing up to 600 pounds, are near the southern shore of the playa. One of these giants furrowed a track 220 feet long when it slid across the playa. Still longer tracks are in the northeastern portion of the Racetrack, one of which is 786 feet long and makes a complete loop and two right-angle jogs. In places, mounds of mud have skidded along, smoothing trails into the mosaic pattern of the playa surface. One such trail starts out two and a half inches wide but ends twelve feet wide. Burro dung, twigs, and 50-caliber cartridges also have made tracks.

The tracks are under study by geologists; they should not

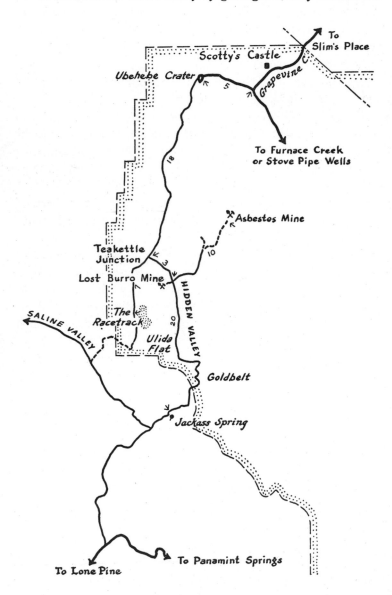

be marred or altered, and although cars may be driven on the Racetrack, they should not be driven across the tracks.

Geologists do not fully agree on what causes the rocks' movement, but it obviously is a natural phenomenon, not a hoax. The human factor can be ruled out. Magnetism and earthquakes, explanations sometimes suggested, are also invalid. Wind is the most probable propelling force. Gusts approaching 80 to 90 miles an hour probably occur in the Racetrack area and are believed sufficient to move even the larger rocks when the playa surface is wet and the rocks imbedded in ice. Ice three inches thick has been observed on the Racetrack, and when the playa is wet its surface, while firm, is slippery enough that a car can be pushed without its wheels turning.

A mile or two beyond the Racetrack is the Lippincott Mine which produced lead used by a Los Angeles battery company. Two and a half miles north of the playa a side road winds down a canyon to the Ubehebe and Copper Bell mines.

Side trips.—HIDDEN VALLEY: Hidden Valley is reached by turning east six miles north of the Racetrack and winding through Lost Burro Gap. The caves in the canyon walls were excavated by University of California archaeologists in 1951. They found basket fragments and bones, indicating that long ago the caves were used by Indians.

ASBESTOS MINE: The mine is reached by turning left at an unmarked intersection about a mile and a half beyond the Gap. The road climbs the eastern slope of Hidden Valley, winds among pinyons and junipers and through a road-cut abounding in fossil fish, to end at the mine situated on the rim of Death Valley.

GOLDBELT: The road continuing straight through Hidden Valley and across Ulida Flat leads to the Goldbelt, an area of intermittent mining. With a truck it is possible to climb Hunter Mountain, cross the ridge, and descend into either Panamint Valley or Saline Valley. A more usual loop trip in truck or jeep is into Saline Valley on the road beyond the Lippincott Mine, near the Racetrack.

GREENWATER VALLEY

Places.—GREENWATER and FURNACE, ghost towns.
Possible side trips.—RYAN and DANTES VIEW.

Possible loop trip. — Across GREENWATER VALLEY, through SALSBURY PASS and JUBILEE PASS, and into southern Death Valley.

Road.—Good desert road readily passable; no steep grades except on some of the side roads near the site of Greenwater. The Salsbury-Jubilee road is oiled.

Map.—Facing page 66.

Suggested time.—Two or three hours for a trip to Greenwater; all day for the loop trip.

Picture ideas.—Desolate GREENWATER, once a booming camp; the view across the Greenwater Basin taken near FURNACE.

Tour.—The GREENWATER VALLEY road, which swings east from the Dantes View pavement, is one of the easier back-country drives, but note the sign warning that the route is seldom patrolled.

The main road to GREENWATER and FURNACE turns east eight miles after leaving the pavement. Furnace is west of Greenwater. The maze of roads can be explored safely.

In 1906 a strip of land along these hills that measured 20 miles long and 10 miles wide was staked with claims. In less than five months' time 2,500 claims were filed at Independence, the county seat. The population jumped from 70 to 1,000 in a month. "The district will have a city as large as Butte, Montana," a newspaper of the day predicted.

Copper was behind the frenzied activity—but it proved only a trace. Shafts were sunk as deep as 1,600 feet but no ore body lay "up, down, or sideways," as publisher Sidney Norman later remarked. Only one shipment of roughly 20 tons was made from Furnace, a camp four miles northwest of Greenwater. The ore was about 20 per cent copper and carried some value in gold and silver.

Greenwater had a post office, a bank, two newspapers and a magazine, telephone and telegraph service, grocery and hardware stores, and "the only drug store in the Funeral Range," according to a 1907 advertisement, and "fresher and better meat than Los Angeles or San Francisco," according to another one. Water was hauled 30 and 40 miles to the camp, and sold for ten cents a gallon. Lumber was hauled in by an 18-horse team. Passengers arrived on the "Death Valley Chug Line," an automotive stage serving Greenwater daily

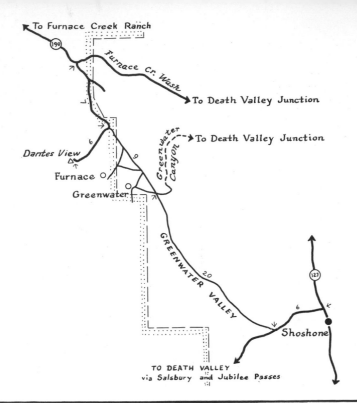

Above: Greenwater

Below: Daylight Pass

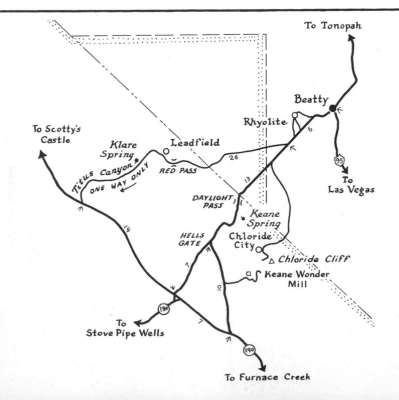

HIDDEN VALLEY Joshua Tree

SALT CREEK

Above: One of the Springs

Below: North along the Creek

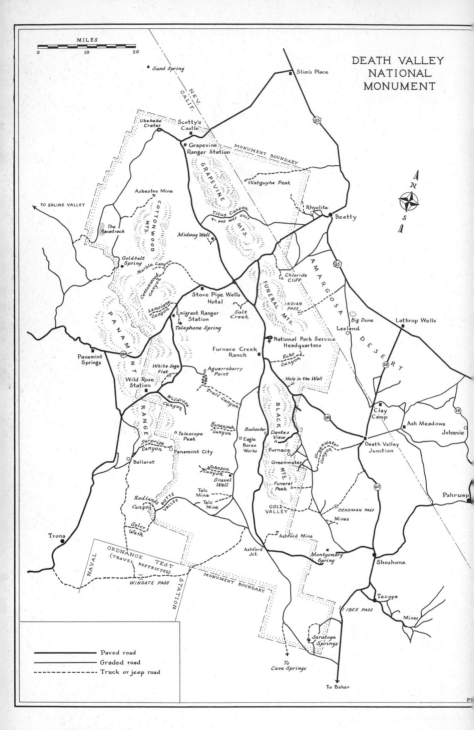

DEATH VALLEY NATIONAL MONUMENT

ROADS (PAVED OR GRADED) AND JEEP AND TRUCK ROUTES

ECHO CANYON Needle Eye

ARRASTRE   Crude Gold Mill

MARBLE CANYON   *Below:* Indian Petroglyphs
                    Right: Marble Canyon Wash

One of the Narrows in Marble Canyon

from both the Tonopah and Tidewater Railroad and the Las Vegas and Tonopah.

Furnace and Greenwater were the largest of several towns in the district. Greenwater was made up of several. First there was Kunze, situated in a canyon with no room to spread out, so its residents moved over the hill and merged with Ramsey. This new camp, bigger and better than its predecessors, was named Greenwater. The *Death Valley Chuck-walla*, published in Greenwater, commented on the moving day: "Saloons and boarding houses, stores and brokerage firms are doing business on both sides of the mountain at the same time. A barkeep puts down his cases on a knoll en route from the old camp to the new one and serves the passing throng laden with bedding and store fixtures. . . . Those who remain in the old camp are walking two miles to the new one to get eggs for breakfast. Those who have journeyed to the new are walking two miles to the old to get their mail."

No buildings are intact at Greenwater now. Some were moved to Shoshone; others have been blown to pieces by the wind. The old Miners Hospital in Furnace served for nearly 50 years as the Shoshone general store, but it is now replaced. The boom towns are marked by little more than scattered bottles, rusty metal, and weathered timbers. Not much machinery is left at the mines; only the shafts and the enormous dumps remain as evidence of the dream of wealth in copper.

THE DAYLIGHT PASS AREA

Places.—Off the highway to KEANE WONDER GOLD MILL; back, and up to CHLORIDE CITY and CHLORIDE CLIFF; on to RHYOLITE; return to the Valley through TITUS CANYON.

Roads.—Not maintained, narrow and rough; steep grades and sharp curves with abrupt drop-offs. All the roads are generally passable for anyone experienced in back-country desert driving. The Park Service has up-to-date information on road conditions.

Map.—Facing page 66.

Suggested time.—All day.

Picture ideas.—The KEANE WONDER tramway silhouetted against the sky; the view from HELLS GATE on a clear day; dug-out houses at CHLORIDE CITY; panorama from

CHLORIDE CLIFF; RHYOLITE; RED PASS at the head of Titus Canyon, with color film; the SYNCLINE at the head of The Narrows in sunlight; the view out the mouth of TITUS CANYON.

Tour.—The road to the KEANE WONDER GOLD MILL angles off from the highway six miles after turning up the southern approach to Daylight Pass. Gold was found at Keane Wonder in 1903, before the more spectacular Bullfrog strike gave rise to Rhyolite. Ore proved up well and in 1907 the 20 stamps of the mill crushed some 1,800 tons a month. Since then the mine has been worked intermittently. In 1954 the old mill timbers were salvaged, leaving little but the foundation and the giant rusted bull wheel.

The mine is on the hillside a mile above the mill. Bunkhouses stand at its mouth and rolls of cable are neatly stacked at the head of the tram. The tunnels are more dangerous than most. The ceilings of great vaults are unsupported, and walls and floors are pocked with frequent stopes and chutes.

North from the mill a road leads to a few small mines and rickety frame houses. It passes mineral springs and pools which are part of a series along the fault that runs the length of the Funeral Range. This water is "juvenile water," issuing from deep within the earth and not affected by rainfall and water table. The road south from the mill winds into a narrow canyon, the site of sporadic mining.

On toward Daylight Pass, HELLS GATE is reached four miles beyond the turn-off to the old mill. It was named in the days of Rhyolite, Keane Wonder, and Skidoo. Teams dropping into Death Valley would snort and toss their heads as the Valley heat struck them here. "Must think they've stuck their noses into the gates of hell," a teamster once remarked. The name stuck.

KEANE SPRING, on a side road two miles long, supplied water for Chloride City on the crest of the Funerals. Water was so vital that a patrolman was hired to walk the pipeline searching for leaks. Ruins of the old pump house remain, and beyond them the road leads to Chloride City. It is passable in a truck or jeep, but is steep and narrow.

A road turning south at the Monument boundary goes to CHLORIDE CITY, which is 15 miles away situated in a 5,000-foot basin just below the crest of the Funerals. A mill and several houses remain in the town. Three houses are partly dug into the bank of the wash and partly built up with rock. This area has been worked longer than most in Death Valley. One of the Ben Hayes scrapbooks, in the Bancroft Library at the University of California, refers to claims here as early as 1863. Small-scale mining is still common.

The view from CHLORIDE CLIFF is regarded by many as the best on the Valley rim. Its parking area is a mile beyond the ruins of Chloride City. The viewpoint is reached by walking two-tenths of a mile along the road and then up the hill, past a mine tunnel. Tucki Mountain and the Dunes are straight across the Valley. The salt flats shimmer white to the south, and the beds of ancient Lake Rogers are to the north.

RHYOLITE is ten miles east of the Monument boundary. The stillness and the shells of buildings do credit to the wisdom of Johnny Shoshone, an Indian who reportedly was given a few dollars and a pair of overalls for his interest in a gold mine that later produced millions. Johnny harbored no bitterness. His comment was: "White man come, make a big fuss, and go away. I still have my overalls."

Shorty Harris, finder of the original strike at Bullfrog, signed away his rights while drunk for a mere one thousand dollars. For years afterward he reveled in the memory of the glorious time he had in Tonopah while the money lasted, treating friends to drinks and food and staking anyone who asked for a loan. A more elaborate version of the celebration has it that he waited till the Tonopah and Tidewater Railroad reached Rhyolite and then, the telegraph being in, wired Los Angeles for a carload of whisky and a carload of eggs. The world's biggest eggnog was Shorty's aim. When the train pulled in, enthusiastic volunteers swung axes to knock heads off whisky barrels, threw in eggs, shells and all, gave a quick stir with their shovels, and drank.

The TITUS CANYON road turns off the highway one and a half miles west of Rhyolite. The canyon is named for Morris Titus who lost his life there while looking for water. He and two partners had left Rhyolite for a prospecting trip in the Panamints. The first two springs they came to were dry, and after two days they were down to 20 gallons of water for the three men and 21 head of stock. Titus decided to push ahead to a spring he knew of in Death Valley. He never returned. A survey party out of Goldfield found the only evidence of him, a note. Reminiscing about its discovery, S. G. Benedict wrote: "When the chief and I were riding up a canyon . . . we came upon his [Titus'] last message to his partners: 'Have gone down the canyon looking for the spring. Have been waiting for you. Titus.' We named the canyon for him."

The road crosses the Amargosa Desert for 12 miles and then climbs RED PASS, a high point in the Grapevines, before descending into the mountain-rimmed basin above Leadfield.

LEADFIELD, three miles below the pass, was mostly a promotion scheme. C. C. Julian, chief promoter, distributed handbills showing steamers approaching the canyon mouth on the Amargosa River and sailing away loaded with Leadfield ore. With that fantasy he lured both investors and residents —as late as 1925!

Ore was poor, around 7 per cent lead, so dumps were salted with ore hauled over from Tonopah. The venture was doomed from the outset. All that remains are mine tunnels (one of them 1,000 feet long) and piles of weathered lumber that once were houses.

Nine miles below the ghost town, the road entering THE NARROWS twists for two miles between sheer 500-foot walls, in places only 15 feet apart. Particularly on the outside of curves, the walls are hollowed and polished by water and gravel that churn down the wash following cloudbursts. Great mounds of gravel spill from high on the canyon rim to its floor; and high-water marks, left by the raging torrents, show 12 to 15 feet above the wash.

The eastern face of a cliff at the head of The Narrows is dominated by a giant SYNCLINE, gray limestone strata bent in a 50-foot U. KLARE SPRING, two and a half miles downcanyon, was the main water supply for Leadfield. During the mining boom someone with an eye for business mounted a 50-gallon drum on a platform and for "25¢ a Shower" doused dusty miners with a little cold water.

The mouth of the canyon is about five miles below Klare Spring. Looking back toward it after reaching the highway (three miles down the fan), the canyon is difficult to pick out because its walls are so close together.

Chapter *10*

Trips by Jeep and Pickup

Many old mine roads impassable for cars are readily traveled in a pickup truck or jeep, and often, particularly in a jeep, it is possible to drive up a wash. No exact directions can be given for most jeep trips; topographic maps, which are the most useful, may be obtained by writing the United States Geological Survey, Federal Center, Denver, Colorado.

All day should be allowed for the following trips unless otherwise noted.

PANAMINT MOUNTAINS

Aguerreberry Point–Trail Canyon.—Jeep for the whole trip; a pickup for driving up Trail Canyon from the West Side road without going all the way through to Aguerreberry Point, in which case this can be a half-day trip.

A mine road turning a mile and a half below the Aguerreberry Point parking area descends into the northern fork of Trail Canyon, past a tungsten mine. Except for one sharp turn, it is an easy road for anyone used to back-country mountain driving. A road junction is reached after passing the mine. The road up the southern fork of the canyon leads to the Morning Glory Mine, an old claim operated from time to time. Above the camp a tramway runs to the mine tunnel. The ore is a complex one known as tetrahedrite, a beautiful mottled silver-gray, blue, and green ore.

Hanaupah Canyon.—Usually passable in a pickup for anyone skilled in rough road driving.

The tracks turn off the West Side road two miles north of Eagle Borax Works, then climb the Hanaupah Fault Scarp and the fan. Just before the mouth of the canyon they drop to the floor of the wash, which is cut perhaps 75 feet. The slope is not as steep as it appears, and will not be a problem in returning. The road actually is not so much off the horizontal as the opposite slope of the wash floor makes it appear.

A burned-out mining camp marks the end of the road. Fine views of Telescope Peak and the surrounding high Panamints may be had by walking uphill from the mine. Beyond the willow tangle at the old camp, a bubbling spring edged with watercress makes a patch of lush green on the dusty brown hillside. At the fork up-canyon from the spring, the southern draw leads to a series of cascades and pools; the northern, to a 25-foot waterfall.

Panamint City.—A truck can usually make the trip easily but current road conditions should be checked before undertaking it.

The road turns off the Ballarat road in Panamint Valley and heads up Surprise Canyon past Chris Wicht's old camp. In 1873 ore was found four miles up-canyon from The Narrows, a bottleneck averaging perhaps 15 feet wide. A year after the strike a town of 1,000 mushroomed in the remote canyon. Silver chloride ore was running as high as $4,000 a ton when United States Senators John P. Jones and William M. Stewart, of Comstock Lode fame, formed the Surprise Valley Mill and Water Company, now memorialized by the brick smokestack towering from the ruins of the mill. Old stone walls remain and a few frame buildings that date from a brief flurry in the 1920's.

Panamint was a wild camp. About 50 fatal shootings occurred during its four-year boom. One look at the town convinced Wells Fargo it should not contract for Panamint bullion; but Senator Stewart was undisturbed. Faced with handling his own shipments, he arranged for open freight wagons to take them down-canyon and across the desert to the railroad—but he first cast the bullion into 500-pound balls, heavy enough that the local highway men couldn't carry them off on their horses. Shipments did not even need an armed guard.

Telephone Canyon.—Jeep; half-day trip to the arch. The jeep road turns off State 190 eight miles southwest of Stove Pipe Wells Hotel and heads toward Tucki Mountain. Three miles after leaving the pavement the road passes Telephone Canyon, with a spur leading off to the south. It is best to park there and walk up the side canyon to an arch a few hundred yards below Telephone Spring. The road threads eight or ten miles farther up the mountain to a mine.

Wingate Pass.—A jeep is needed to go all the way to Panamint Valley although a pickup can cover several miles up the Pass from Death Valley. Much of the area is now included in a Naval Reservation and is closed to public travel.

Wingate Pass turns off the West Side road six miles north of Ashford Junction. It is a broad, open pass, at its summit about 2,000 feet above the floor of Death Valley. Ancient Lake Manly was filled partly by water from the Sierra, which flowed into Death Valley through Wingate Pass.

In the 1880's the 20-mule teams climbed out of the Valley over the pass, and drivers dubbed it "Windy Gap" because there always seemed to be a wind stirring up dust to torment teams and men. Through the years this was changed to Wind Gate, and finally the *d* was dropped.

In 1923 Epsom salts were mined four miles south of the Wingate Pass road and shipped to Trona on a unique monorail. The site of the monorail is reached from a side road that turns off the Wingate road about 22 miles from the West Side road. Little remains of it except an occasional spike or timber.

COTTONWOOD MOUNTAINS

Cottonwood Canyon.—Ordinarily passable only in a jeep, although sometimes compound low gear suffices.

The road turns up the Cottonwood fan west of Stove Pipe Wells Hotel service station, but it is often hard to follow. Occasional cairns along the way topped with white stones indicate the route as an Indian trail to water. An open basin lies a short distance beyond the canyon narrows. Enameled signs still point to once-important springs and trails. The road ends at water in the upper end of the basin, some ten miles beyond The Narrows. It is pleasant to stroll on up-canyon beside the cottonwood-shaded stream. In the late 1800's Indians farmed in the canyon, making use of the year-round water.

Marble Canyon.—Jeep only.

Marble Canyon branches from lower Cottonwood Canyon. No road penetrates it but the wash is usually passable for a few miles. In The Narrows the walls are so close together that it is possible to reach out of the jeep and touch them. Beyond the end of the "road" another gash twists through the mountains for a half-mile, its walls rising smooth and sheer perhaps 100 feet. Petroglyphs are frequent, and so are white men's inscriptions. An "1849" chipped into the southern wall one-quarter mile west of the second narrows is believed evidence that the Pinney-Savage split of the Jayhawker Party left Death Valley through Marble Canyon. The date is much weathered; and near by are the initials "J.B.," which add weight to the theory because there was a Baker in the group.

Lemoigne Canyon.—Pickup or jeep. Half a day is enough unless one plans to go by jeep on up the fork north of the mine, or to hike.

By turning toward the Cottonwoods six miles southwest of Stove Pipe Wells Hotel, it is possible to drive to the Lemoigne Mine, where lead-silver ore has been mined off and on for nearly a century. For years the little rock cabin has been of interest because of someone's sense of humor. Slumped in a dark corner is a suit of clothes artfully stuffed to startle anyone who opens the door.

Grapevine Mountains

North of Wahguyhe Peak.—Pickup nearly to the ridge; a jeep to drop down part way into Fall Canyon on the Death Valley side.

The old topographic map includes this road, but shows it inaccurately. It turns off U.S. 95, nine miles north of Beatty, toward the first canyon north of Wahguyhe Peak. It climbs slowly among huge steel-blue boulders, crossing the bed of the old Rhyolite railway and several north-south roads that belong to the mine boom days. About 24 miles from the pavement it tops the range and offers a view of northern Death Valley framed by pinyon pines. Years ago this was a regular pine nut camp of the Indians, and the site of occasional deer and bighorn hunts.

Funeral Mountains

Gold Dollar Mine Road.—Jeep only; indistinct road.
The old Gold Dollar Mine road picks its way along the

crest of the Funerals south of Chloride Cliff and ends on a cliff above the mine. There is a splendid view of the Indian Pass area from the road's end. The Valley floor cannot be reached from this road.

Echo Canyon.—Four-wheel drive or at least compound low gear is necessary because of loose gravel. It is wise to check on road conditions.

The tracks up Echo Canyon turn toward the Funerals two miles east of Furnace Creek Inn. Shortly after entering the canyon proper, a ten-foot "window" may be seen by looking back at the right-hand wall. The main road (right turn at the fork) leads to the site of Schwaub, a camp that boomed in 1905. Most of the houses that still stand belong to a later date, when the Inyo Mining Company operated the old mines for a time. There is an anticline, an upside-down U in the strata, beyond the camp to the left of the road.

The left-hand fork in the central canyon leads to a maze of roads and a succession of deserted mining camps: one with nothing more than old basements and shattered glass turned purple by the desert sun; another, the Rosair Mine, where one house has a double roof as insulation from the desert heat. This fork of the canyon reaches a high point east of Echo Peak that affords a spectacular view of northern Death Valley. A track turning left high in the central canyon winds to the crest of the Funerals near Nevares Peak, behind Park Service headquarters, and offers a view of the central Valley.

Hole-in-the-Wall.—Pickup or jeep. Two to three hours are enough.

A gap in the foothill wall north of the highway is noticeable five and a half miles up Furnace Creek Wash from the Inn, just above the 1,000-foot elevation sign. A dirt road runs five or six miles through the Hole-in-the-Wall to a travertine quarry which supplied stone for the Pacific Coast Borax Company building on Shatto Place, in Los Angeles.

BLACK MOUNTAINS

Greenwater Valley Country.—A pickup is adequate for most of the roads; a jeep usually is needed to go through Montgomery Pass. This trip can easily be a loop encircling the Black Mountains.

Several roads turn toward the sites of Greenwater and

Furnace, copper camps of 1905, now ghost towns. Few buildings are standing, but occasional timbers, rusted stoves and bedsprings, and mounds of bottles mark the town sites. (See page 66.) The view across Greenwater Valley is one of Death Valley's best.

Eight miles from the Dantes View pavement is a road running north through Greenwater Canyon to Death Valley Junction. Sand may be expected in the wash of the canyon. Several side canyons have petroglyphs (Indian rock carvings) on the walls and one has a series of shallow caves with pictographs (rock paintings), which are rare in Death Valley. The pictographs, in red and black, depict men riding horses and dancing, deer, and bighorn sheep. To the right of the road, farther on, is the Lila C. borax mine, the first in Death Valley to produce colemanite, a rock crystal form of borax.

A side road a mile south of the Greenwater Canyon turn-off can usually be driven in a pickup to a saddle near Funeral Peak, which is the pyramid-shaped peak on the crest of the Black Mountains.

Short mine roads turn off on either side of the main road. Six miles beyond the Funeral Peak turn is a sign pointing to Gold Valley, a scenic mountain-rimmed basin west of the road, where mines were active during the Greenwater boom. The road ends at an old mill at the headwaters of Willow Creek, about four miles beyond Gold Valley. Water usually flows along the creek to a 75-foot cascade, beyond the tangle of trees. Tiny travertine "dams" crisscross the stream.

A mile and a half south of the Gold Valley road, Deadmans Pass road turns northeast past Eagle Mountain, heading toward Death Valley Junction, 21 miles away. Exceptionally smooth desert pavement stretches along the main road just south of the turn.

The Montgomery Pass road runs to a mine, offering a sweeping view of Death Valley, and then drops into Rhodes Wash.

Ibex Mountains.—A pickup can get over most of the roads.

The Ibex Mountains are penetrated by several roads that are interesting to explore. The Southern California Mineral Company operates a large talc mine behind Saratoga Spring, and one road from the mine comes out near the spring.

VALLEY FLOOR

Salt Creek.—Often passable only in a jeep because of sand; current route information is available at Park Service headquarters. Half a day is enough for the trip, although a full day will be rewarding to anyone who enjoys exploring on foot.

The turn off State 190 is marked by a sign about two miles north of the junction with the Daylight Pass road. The ground is too marshy to drive beyond the mouth of the canyon, which is reached about one and a half miles after leaving the pavement. However, walking along the creek a mile or two is worth while.

The inch-long fish in the creek are descendants of fish that lived in Lake Manly during the Ice Age; they have successfully adapted to a changing environment. Killdeer and snipes are common among the grasses and rushes at the water's edge, and often teal are found swimming on a still pool. Coyotes have beaten paths in the salty mud, hunting along the shore for waterfowl.

The road northwest of Salt Creek running to McLean Spring used to be the main route across Death Valley. In 1931 the Salt Creek Trading Post operated at the spring, serving prospectors and venturesome tourists. A canopy of marsh reeds, 10 by 20 feet, was lashed together with wire from the old Rhyolite-Skidoo telephone line. Nearly a century before, the Jayhawkers camped near the spring to smoke the flesh of their remaining oxen before struggling on west afoot.

Mesquite Flat.—Jeep only.

The mesquite hummocks north of the Sand Dunes may be approached from the old road running north beyond the Stove Pipe Wells Hotel service station, or from Midway Well. Parts of the Rhyolite-Skidoo telephone line still stand, and insulators lie half buried in the sand. However, the old line is hard to find because there are no outstanding landmarks.

AMARGOSA DESERT

Big Dune—Leeland.—Readily passable in a pickup; usually all right in a car.

Several dirt roads head south from Beatty across the

77

Amargosa Desert, roughly paralleling the dismantled Tonopah & Tidewater Railroad. Big Dune, a landmark visible
as far away as the Panamint Mountains, is reached by a side
road 20 to 25 miles south of Beatty. Other spurs lead to old
mines and camps, and to stations along the railroad, such as
Leeland. The road joins the pavement north of Death Valley
Junction.

Ash Meadows.—Readily passable; most roads are good
enough for a car. Many unmarked turns make this a con-
fusing area.

A maze of roads crisscrosses the country east of Death
Valley Junction, passing ranches and warm springs and even-
tually ending up in Pahrump Valley where the camps of John-
nie and Pahrump had a brief existence.

There are many ways to explore Death Valley—and much
to explore. Its size and diversity offer limitless possibilities.
It can be seen from a car purring along the highway or a jeep
lurching up the wash of a canyon, from horseback or afoot.
It can be approached from the standpoint of natural history
or human history, or through its scenic or scientific appeal,
or through its photographic possibilities.

Exploring Death Valley, claim those long familiar with
the country, takes more than a week or a month or a year,
more even than a lifetime—but what more absorbing pursuit?

Acknowledgments

The idea for this book first presented itself while my husband and I were stationed in Death Valley, where he served as ranger from 1950 to 1953. Much of the information was acquired then and on repeated trips since; much more is based on the experiences and the knowledge of others.

I am particularly indebted to members of the National Park Service staff in Death Valley who supplied information and, in most cases, read and criticized the manuscript. They include: Fred Binnewies, Superintendent; Lou Hallock, Chief Ranger; Ranger Matt Ryan and his wife Rosemary; Wilbur Alexander, Radio Engineer; Naturalist Ralph Welles and his wife Buddy; and Fred Turner, Naturalist. Herb Maier, Assistant Director of the National Park Service Region Four, and Herb Evison, Chief of Information, Washington, D.C., also gave assistance.

Death Valley "old-timers" who supplied historical anecdotes include Charles Brown (of Shoshone), Lewis Murphy, Ambroise Aguerreberry, Dolph Nevares, John and Mary Thorndike, the late Lon McGirk, Susie Wilson, Agnes Wilson, Dolly Boland, and the late Johnny Shoshone.

The Pacific Coast Borax Company and the United States Weather Bureau supplied information; librarians at the Washington State Library, the Bancroft Library at the University of California, the Inyo County Library, and the Southwest Museum Library at Los Angeles gave freely of their time; and Superintendent Binnewies and Floyd Kellar, former Naturalist, of Death Valley kindly placed the Monument archives at my disposal.

Many books, pamphlets, and periodicals have been drawn upon heavily in an effort to bring together the most salient Death Valley information. Particularly useful were W. A. Chalfant, *Death Valley: The Facts*; G. P. Putnam, *Death Valley Country*; C. B. Glasscock, *Here's Death Valley*; Bourke Lee, *Death Valley* and *Death Valley Men*; and the Federal Writers' Project, *Death Valley Guide*.

The report entitled "Physiology of Man in the Desert," prepared by Dr. E. F. Adolph and associates and published in 1947 by Interscience Publishers, New York, provided most

79

of the information on the effect of heat on men. The weather information came from Arnold Court's paper "How Hot Is Death Valley?" published in the *Geographical Review*, Volume XXXIX, No. 2, 1949, as well as from official records. Parts of the flora and fauna sections are based on the writings of Edmund Jaeger, particularly his *Desert Wild Flowers* and *Our Desert Neighbors*. Much of the material for the geology section came through conversation with Dr. Thomas Clements, geologist at the University of Southern California, and from his booklet *Geological Story of Death Valley*. Charles Hunt of the U.S. Geological Survey was kind enough to criticize the section. Information on Pleistocene man came from Lydia Clements and from her booklet, *The Indians of Death Valley*. Credit for the suggestions on photographing the Monument belongs to Louie Kirk.

I am indebted to Dr. Dick Logan of the University of California at Los Angeles, to John Lamb of the University of Kansas, and to Donna Armstrong and Dave Kapphahn of the National Park Service for reading the manuscript in its entirety; to Dr. Raymond Selle of Occidental College, and to Natt Dodge and Dorr Yeager, Chiefs of Interpretation for the National Park Service, for reading and commenting upon the natural history chapter; and to Dr. William Wallace, archaeologist at the University of Southern California, and his wife Edith Wallace, and to Dr. M. R. Harrington and Ruth Simpson of the Southwest Museum, for criticizing the Indian section of the history chapter.

The several maps in the book were drawn by Patricia L. Theimer.

I am deeply grateful to all of these and many others whom space prohibits listing. Whatever merit this book may have is in a large measure due to their help, while its shortcomings are of course my sole responsibility.

Ruth Kirk

Index